Your Behavior Is Showing

Forty prescriptions for understanding and liking yourself

D1362012

Perry W. Buffington, Ph.D.

HILLBROOK HOUSE
Nashville

ACKNOWLEDGMENTS

My thanks to the wonderful people of Halsey Publishing, publishers of Delta Air Lines' *SKY* Magazine - especially Seymour Gerber, publisher, and my editor, Lidia de Leon. My gratitude to John N. White, manager, promotional media, Delta Air Lines for his creative and editorial direction. Finally, to my former editor, Donna Dupuy, my profound thanks for her ability to see the future and suggest my role in it.

The articles in this volume have been reprinted through the courtesy of Halsey Publishing Company, publishers of Delta Air Lines' *SKY* Magazine.

ISBN 0-929893-00-X

Library of Congress Cataloging-in-Publication Data

Buffington, Perry W.
    Your behavior is showing.

    Includes bibliographies.
        1. Psychology, Applied. 2. Self-help techniques.
I. Title.

BF636.B7444 1988   158'.1   88-24655

DEDICATION

For Sammy, Mike, and Terry

Visionaries who each sought a star — and found it!

For George & Jennifer
So good to see
you again
Dr. Buf.

(12 APR 89)

INTRODUCTION

When I taught at the university level, I constantly reminded my students, "When all else fails, feel free to think, to read, and to change — grow with the new knowledge!" Now that I'm a corporate consultant, I'm continually reminding my clients, "When all else fails, feel free to think, to read, and don't be afraid of change." And as a psychologist, I'm always encouraging people, "Think, read, and find ways to change." Why? Because Your Behavior Is Showing, AND YOU MAY WANT TO CHANGE IT!

In fact, the forty articles in this book, (originally published in Delta Air Lines' in-flight magazine, *SKY*) are designed to do three things: 1. to help you think through and decide on areas of change, 2. to provide new knowledge which leads to the kind of understanding that will facilitate change, and 3. to offer practical steps designed to change undesirable behaviors and develop new, more productive ones.

For instance, do you have some nasty habits you want to change? Are you having trouble getting to sleep at night? Do you want to be more confident? Perhaps you are looking for ways to be more organized? Are you concerned about jealousy, loss of memory, or shyness? Positive change guidelines are all included here!

Are there areas you want to improve? Are you interested in adding more class to your life? Perhaps you would like to improve your intuition, imagination, or luck? Perhaps you want to make positive and lasting first impressions, desire better friends, or you would like to be an expert at something. It's all here, too — hundreds of practical steps designed to help you enjoy life.

So what's the bottom line? There are lots of things which cannot be changed in this world. Fortunately, your own personal behavior can be changed, then YOUR POSITIVE BEHAVIORS WILL BE SHOWING!

Perry W. Buffington, Ph.D.

August, 1988

CONTENTS

Speak Out

Body Trivia

Out of Your Mind

Your Behavior is Showing

Your Behavior Is Showing

Forty prescriptions for understanding and liking yourself

Speak Out

THE ART OF ARGUING

In this modern age of self-expression, differences of opinion and taste are unavoidable. In fact, arguing productively and effectively often results in the emergence of a healthy conversation. However, some personal education is in order.

It is very easy for an argument to manifest itself as aggression. Therefore, you need to know the answers to the following questions: What is an argument? Why do people argue? What are the personality types associated with arguments? Finally, how does one win an argument?

By definition, an argument is a line of reasoning with evidence in support of a personal conclusion. An argument is always an interpersonal event and usually involves more than one person, but it is possible to argue alone. In fact, the most potentially devastating argument is a prolonged altercation within yourself. In this circumstance, there can never be a winner.

There is a great difference between an argument and a discussion. An argument tends to involve two closed minds repeatedly butting against each other. One tries to force the other to yield; the argument becomes a power struggle. A discussion, on the other hand, serves an educative function and is usually less heated, emotionally. Tempers rarely flair during discussions, and the purpose is to learn as much as possible for future use. In a discussion, the point is always remembered; in an argument, the point is often forgotten.

People argue for many reasons, but the most common

theme is power. Whether the conflict is people-centered or issue- centered, the winning point equals power. For one brief, shining moment, the winner is "Number One."

Arguing is also a means to divert thinking. To explain, did you have problems with your spouse before work today? Simple solution: Pick an argument with your co-worker, and your thoughts will be diverted from the scene at home. By focusing invectives on your co-worker, you're spared the pain of uncertainty associated with your spouse's thoughts, feelings and ultimate retaliating actions. Naturally, there is a side-effect. Thirty minutes after the argument with your co-worker, you're going to feel awfully dumb. In your infinite wisdom, you're responsible for having made a scene in an otherwise peaceful work environment, at minimum. You may even lose a friend as a result.

Overall, people argue in order to express themselves, to resolve psychological needs (e.g., power, assertion, emotional release), and to test new ideas. (Of the foregoing, testing new ideas is probably the only healthy reason, since it allows the most room for error.) Finally, there are some people who argue just to hear themselves talk.

When two people are arguing, each of the parties to the argument tends to feed off of and to escalate the other's vehemence and tenacity. In other words, when you raise your voice, the other fighter must become louder. When his volume increases, you become more bellicose just to keep up.

To stop arguing and to remain in control, when your opponent speaks loudly, you should return the volley with a significantly lower voice — or even silence or a whisper. In fact, consider carefully if the other's responses even deserve attention. There is one best point to stop an argument, and that is before it starts.

There are those who will argue that there are only three personality types associated with arguing: the aggressor, the victim, and the instigator. Actually, there are several others. These include the emotional arguer, the overkill specialist, the logician, the clutcher, the manipulator, the internist, and the eclectic.

The emotional arguer desires only to appeal to your heart. There is no intellect associated in his argument, and the more reason you show, the more he will emote. He becomes trapped in pure zest, passion and zeal for the topic. If you don't see it his way, he thinks you are cruel and heartless.

The overkill specialist never truly ends an argument. The topic continues for years and years. If you try to drop an issue, he constantly retrieves it. People like this perpetuate arguments simultaneously, and they never allow you to forget. If they pass you in the hallway, the scene is continued. No setting is safe, and no topic is unapproachable. Their four favorite words are "I told you so" — forever.

The logician is diametrically the opposite of the emotional type. Logicians employ a "Mr. Spock" approach that leaves you speechless. They use reason alone and are masters of fact and trivia. They remain calm throughout the argument and, eventually, force you to lose control. It is very difficult to win an argument with this type of person.

The clutcher, by contrast, never wins an argument. Just when he gets to the final, would-be winning serve, he falls apart, panics, and slowly sinks away. A single nasty glance or a forceful confrontation causes clutchers to sink into the asphalt. They are perpetual victims who spend a great deal of time making apologies.

Manipulators are sneaky. With them, the conversation begins civilly. They will ask your opinion, and a discussion ensues, but before you know it, they've tricked you into an argument. Moreover, you're losing. They take your very own words and twist them around to confuse you. By the time they finish, you aren't sure where you stand on any issue. They take your confusion, and win the argument with your points.

The internist never resolves a struggle. The argument is always personal, internal, and longstanding, and the logic is always circular.

"Why?" questions for which there are never answers are constantly asked. But these questions generate more problems than solutions. Internists never resolve a point and continue to remain at odds — with themselves — for a lifetime.

The eclectic specializes in knowing how to "read" his adversary. He arouses your passion while he engages your intellect. Overkill is not necessary, because "underkill" allows respect for the other person. Logic is applied, where needed. The eclectic possesses the humility of the clutcher and the wit of the manipulator. He hears your contradictions and repeats these inconsistencies to you. As a result, he allows you to hang yourself. Internal struggles are short-lived without his becoming a harbinger of ill will. In short, the eclectic has mastered the subtle art of arguing without resorting to diatribes and other put-downs.

Finally, we come to the question of "How to win an argument." First, an argument must be a last resort — your only hope — so choose it carefully. Negative arguments, unlike those used in debate, are usually spontaneous. If you can see that an argument is imminent, count to ten, or twenty if necessary. If you can, walk away. If you can't, then divert your attention. If you have no choice but to protect yourself from another's attempts to invalidate your opinions and personal worth, then go ahead and argue, following these rules for confrontations:

1. Take a definite position and hold firm.

2. Appeal to the intelligence and/or emotion of your opponent. Appeal to his feelings, emotions, wants, likes and dislikes.

3. If a settlement is not likely, ask your opponent to continue the argument later. Time tends to turn an argument back into a discussion. At that time, when tempers are calm, an arbiter may be appropriate, but be careful here. Placing friends in the middle can precipitate other arguments and lose friends as well.

If you walk away from an argument feeling comfortable, then an argument has not transpired. You have experienced a moment in a relationship where two people have differed and still had appropriate courage to recognize each other's personal worth.

There are no studies, to this researcher's knowledge, on how arguments start, but it is inarguable that people tend to argue about anything and everything. One point on which we can all agree, however, is that the best argument is the one that's avoided.

Reference:
Eisenberg, A.M., & Llardo, J.A. *Argument: A Guide to Formal and Informal Debate.* Englewood Cliffs, N.J.: Prentice-Hall, Inc., 1980.

SMALL TALK

There's nothing small about small talk. And no talk is cheap. Every joke, story, moment of silence, topic of conversation, stutter, or pause says something about you. Although most people believe that small talk or "chitchatting" is an innocuous way of carrying on a conversation without revealing much about themselves, a whole new field of research is suggesting that small talk is a big deal.

For years, small talk has been thought of as nothing more than unimportant, casual conversation. However, the search for the specific link which would more accurately interface man and machine has forced researchers to study even the smallest details associated with human communication. As a result, scientists are convinced that a better understanding of small talk, and conversation rules in general, will provide the insight necessary to create the technology which will allow machines to respond more accurately to the human voice.

In the early 1960s, "conversation analysis," as an area of study, grew out of ethnomethodology — a small, esoteric subset within the field of sociology. This specific branch was designed to study the more mundane details of daily existence. Obviously, chitchatting or small talk qualified.

Currently, the field is small (approximately 30 full-time researchers) with no textbooks available. However, hundreds of scientific papers have been written on the subject, and researchers continue to investigate every possible nuance, sound, and hesitation. Elaborate transcription systems have been developed. Some scholars have analyzed pauses as short as one- tenth of a second. Laughs, jokes, stories, stutters, mispronunciations, and simultaneous utterances are all fair game to the investigators. Finally, after studying thousands of conversations in different settings, researchers have discovered that there is indeed a set of unwritten rules which governs small talk.

Chitchatting guidelines control telephone conversations, barbershop and beautyshop banter, lockeroom talk, cocktail party flirtations, and even boardroom etiquette. Small talk, for example, is essential to the sales profession, and salespeople must master the art. Lawyers are studying small talk to better understand how to frame questions. And the technological community is finding that the bridge between man and machine is governed by the same guidelines that rule in conversations. In other words, small talk has become respectable — and is surprisingly complicated.

Small talk is neither random nor disorderly. It is a highly structured process with a complex set of rules. In fact, chitchatting rules are present in every language, and people follow them without question. In fact, if you ask yourself where you learned these rules, chances are you will not have an answer. They seem so automatic and second nature that people rarely stop and think about it. However, a good look at the rules always makes it easier to understand the object of the game.

Rule Number One: People talk one at a time, in turns. This is so obvious that it sounds like common sense; however, violate the rule, and small talk stops. In fact, other people will walk away from you if you can't play the game, especially in the beginning stages. The ability to take turns with small talk demonstrates how effective you can be when the conversation moves from casual to costly. Interrupting, without waiting your turn, can set you apart from the crowd — usually far away and *very* alone.

Taking turns in conversations has also spurred some competition between the genders. For instance, depending on whom you talk to, when one speaks, the other believes that he or she can't get a word in edgewise. Conversational analysts have studied and answered the question, "Who interrupts more, men or women?"

Many hours of study were necessary to answer this question. Male and female conversation patterns were analyzed in both controlled, laboratory, and everyday settings. Researchers found that males interrupted more than females. In a series of studies, males were responsible for 75 percent of the total number of interruptions. Of course, the researchers point out, this does not address the real question, which involves the *reasons* surrounding the interruptions.

Rule Number 2: Only one person may hold power at a time. The need for power is probably one of the most obvious explanations concerning who interrupts whom. Whoever talks most tends to dominate the other participants in the conversation. Of course, if everyone walks away from the conversation, all power is removed and the game starts over. Power is measured by the amount of eye contact given to one participant, the number of interruptions by the would-be power holder, the amount of time one person spends talking, and (believe it or not) laughter.

Within a conversation, laughter is a shared experience. In essence, one person invites another person to laugh. If the other person doesn't laugh, then power has been taken away from the would-be humorist. Based on this, researchers can evaluate who holds the power — the one who tells the funny story. The other person gives in and surrenders power by laughing.

One study found that physicians avoided laughter for this reason. The study evaluated the relationship between patient and doctor's shared conversations and small talk. Throughout the course of their conversations, patients would attempt to initiate laughter. The researchers theorized that this was done to minimize the power one had over the other or to put both patient and doctor on a more equal footing. In the study, a higher percentage of physicians were disinclined to laugh. This does not suggest that physicians lack a sense of humor, but rather that they may find it necessary to distance themselves. Through distancing, both emotional control and their "perceived" dominance in the relationship is maintained.

As another example, when a child misbehaves, and then tries to make a parent laugh, the child is doing so to reduce the authoritative stance of the mother or father. Small talk, and specifically laughter, is an excellent common denominator that reduces power holders to human status.

Rule Number 3: If for some reason the conversation becomes threatening, order will be re-established. There are many ways this can happen. For example, several people may begin talking at once, or speaking to each other in dyads. When this happens, they will begin to feel anxious. They recognize that they are missing out on another's conversation. As a result of their "need to know," someone will stop talking. Ultimately, the group will come back to talking in turns. That way, every person can hear all that's being said.

Silence also threatens conversations. In fact, if one person is quiet for too long (around 30 seconds), other members of the group begin to fidget. Their gazes shift from floor to ceiling. They move uncomfortably in their seats, or their voices may become higher pitched and louder in an attempt to compensate for the silence. One way or another, someone will start talking, ask questions of the quiet one, and do everything possible to restore the conversation. Usually, persons who are silent are given permission *not* to answer. The group will assume that it is too personal or painful and excuse their nonparticipation. Even if the group does not know why one is silent, they will create an acceptable reason to explain the silence so that the regular group conversation pattern can be restored. It's not unusual for a joke to follow a silence, or another uncomfortable situation. Jokes restore the conversation to an even keel.

Conversation analysts found that small talk is composed of more jokes than stories. The reason: a joke can be told by anybody at anytime; however, a story must fit into the conversation. Once a joke or story is told, it serves to clear the air and restore the conversation. Then the small-talk "rules" begin anew.

Rule Number 4: "Uhs," "ahs," and "wells" are fair tactics to avoid unpleasantries. No conversation can be kept positive all of the time. Conversation analysts have found what psychologists have known for years: humans will delay pain as long as they can.

Other than physical discomfort, most of us fear the hurt of rejection most of all. If you are afraid to ask someone to do something, believing that the answer will be no, your conversation will be filled with "ahs" and "uhs" until you muster the courage to make your request. You may even restart the sentence several times, stutter, or walk away. In other words, the pauses between words, filled with resonant sounds, are a delaying tactic to avoid a response you do not want to hear.

For example, notice the following the next time someone phones. If, after the initial small talk pleasantries and mundane expressions, conversation momentarily stops, and the other party begins with an "ah," what immediately follows is the real reason he or she called.

The rules of small talk apply in all other conversational situations. As relationships move from casual to personal to intimate, the guidelines stay the same. Not only can small talk begin relationships, it can end them. Never forget that small talk is inextricably tied with the all-important first impression.

Most of all, do not minimize the value of small talk. All relationships, from simple friendships to complicated corporate mergers, start with small talk — and big hopes.

References:
Baker, R. Small talk. *New York Times Magazine*, August 19, 1984, *133*, p. 18.

Beinstein, J. Conversations in public places. *Journal of Communication*, 1975, *25*, pp. 85-95.

Roark, A.C. Structure discovered in chitchat. *Los Angeles Times*, November 20, 1986, Section I, *105*, p. 1ff.

HUG ME

Name a many-faceted, many-splendored human expression which is as personalized as a smile. Here's an extra hint: Look around the airport and watch how loved ones greet each other. The closer we get to a major holiday season, the more people openly show their regard for others. After all, "Tis the season" for holiday hugs.

Although linguists do not know the derivation of the word "hug," the meaning is universal, and the behavior has been around a lot longer than the 16th Century when the title formally appeared. Since that time, "hugs" have appeared in the works of Shakespeare, Dickens, Swift, and many others. Moreover, the early 1900s found "hugs" cropping up in women's clothing (e.g., "hug-me-tight," a short, close-fitting woman's jacket) and varieties of engineless buggies. Today, we have "bunny" and "bear" hugs, and infinite variations in between. But the ultimate hug therapy is a product of the 1980s.

With so many self-help books on the market, it's surprising this holiday topic has been omitted. There are hundreds of books to help you understand your personality via astrology, music, biorhythms, color, body shapes, and language. However, to this scientist's knowledge, no one has attempted to diagnose personality styles based on a person's hugging technique.

Before discussing psychotherapeutic hugs or specific forms of embrace, some simple observations are in order. Look around you in the airport lobby. Notice how those "long-lost" females greet each other as one of them is seen deplaning. No hesitation — an immediate embrace and kiss. Of course, the children aren't left out; they're immediately grabbed and caressed. The men, on the other hand, slap each other on the back, grant each other a half embrace (one-arm as opposed to two), and disengage quickly. They probably knew you were watching.

Think about it. If I asked you to give acceptable instances when females may embrace females, females are allowed to hug males, or both genders hug children, you could think of many appropriate times and places. But just how socially acceptable is it for men to embrace? Three occasions: the death of a loved one, a win in an athletic event, and selected holidays. At other times, it's a cultural "no-no."

Perhaps one reason embraces are not readily seen is because holidays, which grant a license to love your fellow person, are too far from one another. After all, it's ten months from Valentine's Day to Christmas. Obviously a committee planned the calendar because most loving holidays (Thanksgiving, Christmas and St. Valentine's Day) are bunched together at the end of the year and the first part of the new year. As a result, you have to wait at least three months for Mother's and Father's Day. Finally, Thanksgiving comes along five months later and allows you to exercise your positive emotions again.

Perhaps another reason is that people have not been taught the proper embracing techniques. This is obviously true in that people have trouble embracing new jobs, knowledge, common principles, goals, or their fellow person. The procedure is simple. If you would like a trial run, practice with your pillow. First, extend both arms horizontally to the floor. Allow someone to step between arms. Clasp arms around each other. A slight (or moderate, depending on skill level) squeeze is in order; the number of pats on the back is optional. Release embrace. Finally, for added practice remove pillow and practice with person in the adjacent seat.

As a faithful observer of "huggers" and "huggees," embraces can be divided into seven distinct art forms. Although the physical technique of an embrace (described earlier) is virtually the same for each, the mental or thought processes underlying this act are qualitatively different.

For instance, take the "lone hugger." This person likely has a fear of closeness. As a result, he rarely shares himself with anyone else, and his embraces are limited to his own arm reaching around his own body. When things become too close, he runs away embracing tightly his own identity.

"The space invaders," are exactly the opposite. They are

textbook clinging vines who hang all over you. They constantly invade your territory or personal space, allowing you little
time to yourself. To paraphrase, "If they can't cling to the one
they love, they cling to the one they're with."

One of the most fascinating is the "political hugger." Just
like countries who appear to embrace each other, and then
proceed to take everything the other owns, they're sneaky.
They make you think you're the most wonderful person in the
whole world. When they're finished with you, you're dis-
posable.

"The fair-fight hugger" picks a fight with you, then feels guilty afterwards. To alleviate his own bad feelings, he insists on
embracing you as tangible proof that you still love him. To the
"fair-fighter," the hug represents resolution or truce. Then,
they start again.

Everyone needs support from time to time, and the "poor
baby hugger" will always come to your rescue. The way you
know you have a "poor baby" on your hands is that "poor babies"
are constantly saying, "Now, now, things will be better. Please
don't worry. Tell me about it" and/or "It's always darkest before
dawn." These folks suffer from perpetual "silver-lining
syndrome." However, on occasion they serve a valuable purpose because they are usually expert listeners and allow you
ample time to vent frustrations. Getting through their "sticky
rhetoric" is the tough part.

"The Saturday night huggers," excited about the "fever" of
the moment, begin early in the week planning their exploits for
the evening. Their partners, typically short-term, are used sel-
fishly to gratify personal pleasures and egocentric whims. For
the sake of delicacy, the discussion of the "Saturday night hugger" is curtailed, and the reader is free to draw his own con-
clusions.

Finally, the "love hugger" represents the Zenith of human
growth. This type of hug is characterized by a "quiet time"

during the embrace. During this silent, unselfish, reflective moment, nothing is required of either person, and no psychological tricks are played. Rather, a pure, emotional commitment and love is expressed.

The rumor around psychological circles is that "hug therapy" is catching on. Obviously, there is a relationship between embracing and improved health, because one of the side-effects of hugs is a reduction in personal stress. Hug therapy goes one extra step beyond laughter and simple touching. As a result, support is gleaned each time you are embraced. The warmth and closeness of another person implies that you are worthwhile. By being a huggable person, you take care of yourself, increase feelings of self-worth, and generate warmth and closeness to others.

For instance, library workers at a major university were instructed to touch accidentally the hands of individuals while checking out books to them. By design, the touch was so lightly administered that few might even consciously know they were touched. Outside the library, a roving reporter stopped and interviewed students. Those who had been touched acknowledged much warmer and more positive feelings toward the library, themselves, and life in general than those, who in a control group, had not been touched. The point is if a touch facilitates such positive regard, imagine the potential of a sincere embrace.

A hug alleviates (albeit temporarily) loneliness. This premise has been put to test (informally) in pain clinics. Chronic pain patients have little fun in life and often exhibit thoughts of helplessness and feelings of depression. It is believed that simple, physical contact with another is an effective agent in reducing the emotional components of pain. At least while you're receiving a sincere, loving hug, your thoughts are diverted away from your problems, worries, and other hurts.

Embraces are a way to share your identity, to offer support, and to give reassurance. The main misconception about hugs is that they are more effective with children than adults. Not true. They are as effective and work equally as well with all persons. Try it. It'll make you grow big and strong emotionally.

BEST FRIENDS

Let's take a good look at friendships. If Abbott had not had Costello, he wouldn't have been as funny. Luke Skywalker would have had to be considerably more careful in battling the Empire if his friend, Han Solo, had not been there. Sherlock Holmes would have missed numerous nuances without his Dr. Watson. Buffalo Bob wouldn't have been the same without Howdy Doody. And so on...

But how do friendships, and familial ties, grow and mature? To say that our most important relationships need nurturing and undivided attention to ensure smooth sailing is an understatement. Simply put, you can't survive without friends.

You may never have really thought about how you pick your pals, but some social psychologists have spent lifetimes studying what makes a friend a friend.

One point upon which all psychologists agree (a rare feat in and of itself) is that men and women are gregarious beings. We have a need for affiliation. This need to get to know and to be with others is the social glue that creates families and civilizations. When people are anxious, they huddle together for support.

A very famous psychological study of the late 1950s proved this point.

A social psychologist led a group of participants to believe that they were going to receive a shock. Some were told that the shock would be mild, and others were told that it would be painful. When they were asked if they wanted to wait alone or with friends, those who expected a painful experience preferred to wait with others. In general, "misery loves company" — but only when the company is just as miserable. Comparing intellectual and emotional notes along with behavioral actions helps to reduce anxiety about the unknown.

The old adage, "Birds of a feather flock together," is true when it comes to selecting your friends. You are immediately attracted to those who are good-looking, for example. It would appear that physical appearance is a major criterion for interpersonal attraction. In computer dating services, it has been found that physical appearance is a central factor in determining an individual's choice of a dating partner.

Although beauty is in the eye of the beholder, most people prefer individuals who are slender. Tallness is an asset for men, but not for women. Women prefer men with broad shoulders and a tapering waist. But one of the more striking points is that brunettes are perceived as more attractive than blondes or redheads.

We have a tendency to rate those who come in pretty packages on a more positive basis. It is as if we expect them to be more competent and productive than their less seemly counterparts. For instance, if you were sitting on a jury, you would tend to disbelieve that an attractive person could commit the crime in question. Basically, that's why attorneys make sure their clients look good in court. Psychologists refer to this as "face validity." Actually, the term refers to anything that is packaged properly. The first impression implies that "this is good stuff."

Back to the courtroom. Even if you finally begin to believe that the accused individual was in fact guilty, an attractive person who is found so will tend to receive a lesser sentence. In addition, attractive people are perceived as more talented and are expected to be more adroit in social skills. We like glitter.

At the risk of paraphrasing another platitude, "If it glitters, it must be gold."

In short, we are likely to select those friends who are similar to ourselves in attractiveness. That means that extraordinarily beautiful people tend to have fewer friends because "average-looking folks" won't try and develop a friendship due to fears of rejection and personal perceptions of inadequacy.

We have a major fear of rejection by those whom we perceive to be more attractive than us. It is as if we fear rejection as the ultimate "put down." This fear keeps us from developing friendships with those whom we consider to be more competent, more fashionable, more intellectual... more of everything that we don't have. As a result, you irrationally say to yourself, "They wouldn't be interested in me. I don't have anything to offer this relationship." Because of these fears, both parties in question sit at home and watch television. (Beauty can be a curse.)

Even though one tends to select a mate or a friend who is perceived to be an "attractive equal," once married or entered into a strong friendship, you will tend to rate your buddy as more attractive than you are. Many people grab any opportunity to take their self-esteem, reduce it to nothingness, and bury it. To resurrect your opinion of yourself, just remember that the other person is probably thinking that you are more attractive than he or she is.

There is another factor that's important in selecting friends. We are attracted to those individuals who are similar to us attitudinally. We are more attracted to those who share our likes and dislikes in any area. Take a good look at your best friends at work; you enjoy their company because most of the time you agree on things. Now, if your best friend happens to be gorgeous and share your same attitudinal whims, then you probably have a friend for life. The research is suggesting that physical attractiveness and attitude are equally important in selecting friends.

So far, attractiveness and attitudes have been the forerunners in establishing relationships, but there are other factors also. Take "complementarity," for instance. There are times when opposites do attract. Take the busy executive who is constantly anxious, inordinately productive, but will not allow a moment to slow down. Perhaps that person should select a friend who is rather "laid back" or lacking in motivation. In this instance, opposite roles provide each other with certain benefits. It's the old "every comic needs a straight man" philosophy. That simple technique made Burns and Allen successful.

Then there's the concept of reciprocity. To explain: if you like me, then you must have excellent taste and judgment. Salespeople have understood this concept for years. Most people who want to start a friendship with someone usually begin by praising the target. The salesman will say, "It's a beautiful home you have — now let me show you the vacuum cleaner." The compliment is used to get the foot in the door.

When people are praised, they become more susceptible to the message that is being delivered. Those who are admired and praised tend to return these feelings. Simply put, when someone pays you a compliment, you wonder why you haven't paid them more attention. After all they like you; you can't be all bad. Then the cycle is set in motion. A relationship is based on a *quid pro quo* of compliments, and reciprocity of regard helps maintain the friendship — and sell the vacuum cleaner.

We tend to select friends who are accessible. This psychological law is called "propinquity." It's common sense psychology. We tend to be more attracted to those individuals with whom we have frequent contact. This is the effect of nearness. In an apartment complex, the likelihood of developing a friend who's next door is much greater than one who's several buildings over. The routine of seeing another person on a day-in and day-out basis sets up the possibility of a friendship.

In addition to physical attractiveness, complementarity,

reciprocity, and propinquity, people like to have friends who are "hard to get." Having a friend whom everyone else wants but doesn't have makes you "special." These friends are more positively valued and make great conversation at cocktail parties. When you state that your friend (who everyone knows is powerful and influential), says you should invest in a certain stock, the room suddenly becomes very quiet. You are the center of attention — just because you have a friend who is "hard to get."

There is also another phenomenon which some parents have found out (the hard way) tends to cement relationships. It is called the "Romeo and Juliet Effect." If your parents actively oppose a potential mate, you will likely date them more. The parental opposition tends to intensify feelings between couples. This only has an effect during the first six to ten months of the relationship. During the early stages, parental opposition tends to exacerbate needs for security, and as a result the couple clings together more strongly.

Finally, just like people who are too attractive, those who are too competitive tend to scare us even more. If you are one of the proud few who is indeed superior in all areas, it is probably to your advantage to err occasionally. You see, if there's a choice between someone who is superior and clumsy and another who is only superior, the former will win every time. The occasional mistake-maker will be judged as more human and less threatening, and potentially a more valued companion.

So, your best friends will stay your best friends if they are somewhat attractive, don't threaten your views on world peace, round out your rough edges, are nearby when you need them, and maintain their standing as "gems in a world of zircons." Now, if you can take these ingredients and add to them honesty, sincerity, and a mutual positive regard, then you may have a friend for life.

References:
Schachter, S. *Psychology of Affiliation*. Stanford, California: Stanford University Press, 1959.

THE GENTLE ART OF SHARING SECRETS

Chances are if this article begins with the promise of sharing little-known psychological truths which will give you power over personal and work-related problems, you will find yourself reading rapidly and intently. Fortunately, this article does just that. But if these points were divulged now, reading would stop. First point: Secrets have value.

If this article shares information about close friends, the probability of your reading further and more sharply increases. Second point: Secrets offer understanding.

If this article shares personal secrets about you, it will be read and re-read several times. Third point: Secrets are kept from ourselves.

Humans thrive on secrets, because they serve to unify a friendship or to give one a competitive edge over neighbors. As a result, one feels more in control. To illustrate, consider how vulnerable you felt the last time you thought, or heard someone else say, "That person knows too much." Consider further the childhood taunts of "I know something you don't know, and I won't tell." Remember how badly you thought you "needed" this information. Then, when finally told, how you felt special and privileged. Later, when the secret was overheard from another, it was an "ego trip" to say, "I already knew that."

Since childhood, things have hardly changed. TV shows like *Dallas* (Who Shot J.R.?), *The Secrets of Midland Heights,*

Secret Storm, talk shows, and other entertainment values all intrigue via secret and partial information. The desire to know information available only to a few captures and consumes one's immediate interests. If the information is not readily attainable, the desire may become long-term. Humans also tend to remember those things which are not completed or not readily accessible longer than those which are, and in the process, assign more importance to them.

Secrets, not only used for entertainment, are necessary for economic and psychological support. Major corporations, governments, and other kinds of organizations must maintain secrecy to protect themselves from competitors, thereby maintaining their financial and structural autonomy. Individuals do the same for emotional survival. For instance, the following words, "Will you protect my confidence?" can be reassuring or frightening. They're reassuring when mutual trust is present; frightening when second thoughts prompt re-evaluation of the person's integrity with whom one has shared.

Anxiety and fear follow when one believes his individual privacy has been jeopardized. As a result, the simple desire to share with another has become complicated.

On the surface, a secret would seem to be a simple, straightforward matter. But, as one soon discovers, the "secret" concept is intrinsically bound up with the explosive, complicated issue of personal privacy. In fact, at no previous time has valued privacy been more threatened than now. Modern life finds media, environmental, health and legal intrusions to be common and pervasive. As a result, the desire for personal secrecy has attained an ever-higher standard, and the ability to keep a secret entrusted by a friend is not only a skill, but a personal tribute. Regrettably, the ability to keep a secret is often taken for granted.

The psychology of secrecy is one area which has not been systematically studied, but social scientists do know the personality traits which must be observed before an individual will share secrets with another. The recipient, or trusted person, is one who is highly influential, attractive, and nearby. In addition, the presence of attitudinal commonalities — similar likes and dislikes - between the two parties increases the likelihood that a secret will be shared. Finally, one tends to trust others who are willing to take responsibility for their actions rather than blaming another for misfortunes.

The process of evaluating these attributes and establishing a trust relationship begins, like any other, with surface contact and conversation. This consists of initial banter (e.g., weather, family, job) where the potential for friendship is evaluated. The prospect for a meaningful relationship begins when attitudinal comparisons suggest similarities which minimize threats, fears and intimidations.

The thought process is as follows: "That person's a lot like me, so he'll understand my situation." Following initial and subsequent conversations, if both parties choose, friendship or "mutuality" commences and grows: the "we" stage.

As the dyad progresses, people recognize complementary strengths in others which are missing in themselves. The greater the complementarity, the stronger the friendship; as a result, a deeper, more honest exchange of values, secrets and true feelings results: the trust phase. As an individual views another as "safe," secrets begin to flow, since safety implies that a trust will not be violated.

The relationship is strengthened each time one party shares with the other, who acknowledges receipt of the information, and adds to the conversation with comments like, "I've felt the same way," or "I've done the same thing." But if the trust is destroyed, the degree of anger which follows is a direct result of wondering 1. "How much does that person really know about me?" and 2. "How much can this information damage my credibility?"

To simplify, if a pseudo-friend who is aware of another's intimate concerns and secrets breaks confidence, ensuing anger and hate prepares the victim for combat and covers an emotional hurt. If numerous secrets are violated by several acquaintances, the capacity to trust others suffers, and the hurt individual may become "over-closed" or too alone. But the question remains: "Why do people share secrets and risk being hurt?"

Allowing others to know your secrets appears to have many cost- benefit features. To begin with, secrets, when kept, tend to solidify relationships. The closeness of a friendship is embodied in the trust between the two parties. As one shares with the other, and disclosures are reciprocated, a cycle of positive regard cements the friendship. The sharing of secrets also tends to nurture all parties psychologically and emotionally. For instance, the imparting of secrets serves as an anxiety reducer, particularly if the secret concerns a traumatic event. Worries and concerns are aired, providing a temporary tension reducer.

Another reason for sharing secrets is to seek education, clarification and alternatives from another source. The information learned from a "What would you do if..." secret is a more effective and longer-lasting anxiety reducer, particularly if alternatives are implemented promptly.

Probably the most common reason why confidants are sought is a desire for closeness with an important other. Humans are naturally gregarious; the desire to know, to understand and to love another satisfies security, safety and companionship needs. By allowing another to know one's secrets, a trust is acknowledged not only with the friend, but with oneself. However, people sometimes have difficulty informing themselves about their own secrets.

When one ponders the use of secrets, one immediately thinks of either sharing or keeping things from others. However, it is not unusual to keep secrets from oneself, particularly if one feels emotionally incapable of dealing with the problem. Such secretiveness may be voluntary or involuntary.

This is not as unusual a phenomenon as it sounds. People secretly protect themselves from threatening situations which would force one to admit inadequacies. The following are examples: A friend who was forced to endure a tragic event, and now has little or no recall of the episode; an unprepared college student who is failing and blames the professor's teaching method; an adult whose parents abandoned him and has blotted out portions of childhood years; a colleague who is having major marital problems, and secretes this information by working longer and longer hours; or Aesop's fox who cannot reach the grapes and decides that they probably are sour anyway.

Then there are extreme cases where a split personality is present. Within the individual, the two or more distinct personalities which emerge are usually secret from each other. Each ego faction has its own memories, behaviors and social relationships. (Such cases so intrigue the public that *The Three Faces of Eve and Sybil* became best-sellers.) This leads to the obvious point that secrets can protect from emotional hurt, and are certainly very human. However, tricking oneself via secrets as a way of dealing with every problem is certainly not in one's best interests. Self-secrets may delay, and at times that is necessary, but secrets rarely erase problems.

Finally, there is one other individual quality of secrets which is rarely discussed. The secret's owner is the holder of a great deal of power and control. That is, a secret can never be taken away from an individual until that person chooses to surrender it. Once a secret is told, a gamble begins because total ownership of power has been surrendered. So trading secrets is tantamount to trading personal power.

Secrets are entirely human and not exclusive to modern times. Personal secrets separate one from the masses and may offer a competitive edge. They have value, often provide insight in human interactions and cement trust relations. As a result, there is no better feeling than the ensuing camaraderie, or no worse emotion than the aloneness perceived when a trust is violated.

The ability to keep secrets is a gentle art. Gentle, by definition, in that protecting one's trust is rarely flamboyant. Who is most likely to keep and to protect a friend's secret? Very simply, the person who values another's friendship and companionship above all, and who can sequentially place someone else's needs before his own. Perhaps human understanding is the greatest secret of all...

LASTING IMPRESSIONS

First impressions have become rather automatic in our daily lives. In less than four minutes of almost subconscious thought, we can determine if another person is beautiful or handsome, emotionally stable, or intellectually competent. What's more, first impressions are usually assumed to be infallible.

The truth about first impressions is that they can lead to a case of mistaken identity, and most people will not take the time to reformulate a second or third impression. They stick by a first opinion, whether it's right or wrong. Fortunately, there are ways to minimize the risk of being victimized by another person's incorrect first impression of you. In fact, understanding why we need to make good first impressions, common errors associated with them, and techniques which minimize projection of an erroneous first impression can make your first impact on others a positive and lasting one.

The psychological reasons underlying first impressions are

not very complex. When a person is introduced for the first time, there is no frame of reference or former impressions to rely on. So, one is immediately created. As a result, it has enormous impact and becomes the standard by which that person, event, or situation is judged on future occasions. Psychologists refer to this as the "primacy effect."

To demonstrate this, a classic study conducted in the late 1950s still holds true. Participants were asked to read two different, fictitious paragraphs about a man identified as "Jim." In one paragraph, he was portrayed as friendly; in the other passage, the opposite. After reading the material, participants were asked their first impression of Jim.

Of those who read the friendly passage, 95 percent stated that their first impression of Jim was positive. Of those who read the unfriendly description, only three percent stated that their first impression was positive. Then came the psychological twist.

The researchers wanted to know what happened when the same participant read both paragraphs, one after the other. One group of participants would read the friendly paragraph and then immediately read the unfriendly one. The other group would read the same two passages, starting with the unfriendly one. Here's what the researchers found.

Of those who read the friendly-unfriendly sequence, 88 percent rated Jim as friendly. Only 12 percent were swayed by the negative paragraph. Of those who read the unfriendly passage first, 82 percent stated that their first impression of Jim was negative. What was read first had a profound impact (the primacy effect) on the individual who was formulating an initial impression.

There's no doubt that the primacy effect is powerful and resistant to change; however, there is a way to alter a first impression, and psychologists call this the "recency effect."

Researchers in the study previously cited sought a way to

reduce the power of the primary impression. To achieve this, they followed a similar experimental format and continued to present both positive and negative reading passages to the participants. However, instead of immediately presenting one paragraph followed by another, they allowed time to elapse between the reading of the first and second paragraphs. They found that time was effective in changing first impressions.

Based on their findings, they concluded that as memories fade, recent information takes precedence and becomes a new standard by which present and future impressions are evaluated and reformed.

As a corollary to these findings, the researchers suggested another powerful way to affect first impressions. They suggested (almost tangentially) that simply counseling individuals — encouraging them to avoid snap judgments and to weight the evidence before they form an opinion — could also be an effective deterrent to erroneous first impressions. This is a more profound suggestion than the earlier researchers believed.

A recent study tested this idea and verified that monitoring one's thoughts prior to formulating a first impression does have an impact. The study required people to be accountable for their impressions.

The participants were 72 college students who evaluated evidence from criminal cases. They were asked to assess a defendant's guilt or innocence. Similar to earlier studies, positive vs. negative information was supplied about the alleged criminal.

Consistent with the previous study, individuals who were given the positive information followed by negative feedback tended to see the defendant as innocent. Those given the negative data first were more likely to assess the defendant as guilty. This occurred only when the subjects were allowed to keep their reasons to themselves. The surprise came when they were asked to explain why they thought the person was guilty or innocent.

When subjects were expected to justify their opinions, order of presentation of evidence (positive vs. negative) made no difference. By requiring the individuals to pay attention to their thoughts, to be vigilant in the assessment of data, and to be prepared to defend their opinions, the primacy effect lost its hold.

One additional side result of this study was that the participants' recall of details improved. By dealing with facts exclusively, they were not as prone to make the typical errors associated with first impressions.

The three typical mistakes in judgment are 1. "halo" or "horns," 2. logical, and/or 3. leniency errors. The halo or horns errors stem from our tendency to evaluate people in a general sense as "good" or "bad." If we view them positively, then we mistakenly assume that everything they do is positive. If we perceive them negatively, then we tend to assume that they have negative traits and characteristics. The boss who likes a particular employee has difficulty finding fault with his or her work. A favorite football figure is rated favorably overall, even when he fumbles the ball. People we like can do no wrong, and vice versa. The possibility of making this error is present when we formulate any first impression.

Logical errors are common, and no one is exempt from committing them, especially when it comes to first impressions. There is a personal-experience component in operation with logical errors. We have been taught that certain personal traits go hand in hand with others — even if there is no evidence to support the view.

For example, if a person stands up for his or her rights, one may also assume that he or she has a strong character. Or people who are attractive tend to be seen as intelligent, sociable, and competent. Of course, the fact that a person is aggressive or good-looking is no guarantee that other traits will be present also. Ascribing traits we do not see based on one observed behavior is a logical error which leads to erroneous first impressions.

The third common mistake in judgment is usually the result of trying to give another person the benefit of the doubt. Simply put, leniency errors happen when people desire to make as many positive judgments as possible and avoid negative ones. This error is prominent in situations which require a person to state what they have observed publicly. A leniency error is forthcoming when a person prefaces a remark with "What you did wasn't all that bad" or "Compared to how others would have handled it..." Leniency errors influence our first impressions, especially when a person wants to be liked and needed by everyone.

Although psychologists have explored the value of first impressions, the role of primacy and recency, the need for personal accountability as one formulates impressions, and common errors, there is one question which has still not been answered: Why is it that occasionally two people meet for the first time and hit it off right away? Or the converse: Why is it that two people meet and immediately dislike each other? There really is no definitive answer to either question, but there are clues.

There are many ideas concerning instant attraction, running from the psychological to the metaphysical. Psychologists suggest that it is possibly a combination and interaction of three critical ingredients: 1. facial expressions, 2. good looks, and 3. level of self-esteem.

Facial expressions and good looks immediately draw one to a person. There's no doubt about it — everyone enjoys looking at other individuals who are expressive and attractive. However, if these two ingredients are present along with a level of self-esteem similar to (or slightly higher than) our own, we will tend to like this person and be attracted to him or her almost immediately. But to be totally honest, there really is no answer which explains one's immediate attraction to someone else. In fact, answering this question might take the mystery out of this special type of first attraction.

In general, there are several ways to enhance first impressions.

1. Create a positive image. Neatness counts, and it can be manufactured. Know which clothes look best on you and add to your wardrobe accordingly. Utilize good grooming techniques which accentuate your features.

2. Greet the person you are meeting for the first time with a firm handshake, direct eye contact, and a smile. Determine the person's name who is being introduced to you and make it a point to refer to him or her by name at least three times throughout the course of the conversation.

3. Start and end the initial meeting with a positive remark. This will engage both the primacy and recency effects so that you can use them to maximum advantage.

4. Listen attentively, as if someone were going to ask you to substantiate your personal opinion. This will help you keep judgment errors to a minimum. Before concluding a discussion or meeting, summarize out loud the points discussed. This is a direct statement of positive interest to the other person.

5. Emphasize — but not to the point of bragging — your own abilities and accomplishments. If the listener is prone to make a halo, logical, or leniency error, then it will be in your favor. He or she will attribute other abilities to you as well, without your having to point them out.

First impressions are inevitable. They are like a first page in a mental filing system. As a result, each time the file is opened, the initial impression is reread. The point to remember is that you can almost always project a positive first impression. Although it takes effort and consistency over time, the results can be impressive.

References:
Luchins, A. S. Primacy-recency in impression formation. In C.I. Hovland (ed.), *The Order of Presentation in Persuasion.* New Haven, Conn.: Yale University Press, 1957.

Tetlock, P. E. Accountability and the perseverance of first impressions. *Social Psychology Quarterly,* 1983, *46*, pp. 285-292.

Body Trivia

A TWO-HANDKERCHIEF TOPIC

Sneezing is, among other things, certainly one form of personal expression which happens with little predictability and much individual variation. Many visibly enjoy the sneeze; others are embarrassed. All usually say, "Excuse me," implying some form of cultural sanction which requires forgiveness. Moreover, sneezing may be a kind of "last frontier," as there is little psychological or medical literature to augment one's knowledge of this phenomenon. (One encyclopedia devoted a mere three lines to the sneezing process.)

The sneeze does not appear to vary from one culture to another, or sociologists surely would have produced volumes on the topic. We were unable to locate a fancy, multi-syllable name for it, but the noise produced by a sneeze is called a sternutation. To date, no one has had a sneeze named in his or her honor. Finally, the individual owner of a sneeze rarely introspects as to the inward and outward physiological manifestations involved.

To prove the point, conduct the following experiment: On the next occasion of a sneeze, rush immediately to a mirror and stand in front of it. Now, as you sneeze, keep both eyes open and watch the process. You may want to observe, but your reflex system doesn't allow it. So, for the faithful — or casual — observer of sneezes and sneezers, some scientific documentation of the "sneeze process" is in order.

Whether your sneeze is delicate, moderate or flagrant, there are several common scientific points. Much like other mysterious, but practical, bodily wonders, sneezing serves a very valuable purpose: the process expels unwanted material from the nasopharynx or closely adjacent air passages. If the local musculature seeks to expel particles unaided, the result is choking or gagging.

The respiratory system may contribute a blast of air resulting in a full-blown sneeze. The vocal cords are kept shut until chest pressure is sufficiently strong; then air is suddenly allowed to escape upward. To elaborate, sneezing is a respiratory reflex which manifests as an involuntary, audible spasmodic inspiration of air followed by a violent expiration of air through the nose and mouth.

The field of pneumatometry informs that the pressure force of the sneeze results in a highly atomized naso-oral discharge of which spray droplets 0.1 to 0.2 millimeters in size are hurled at a speed of thirty meters (over 90 feet) per second for a distance of 0.5 to 1.6 meters (roughly 1 1/2 to 4 1/2 feet).

The greatest "sneeze speed" recorded found expelling particles moving at 167 kilometers per hour (103.6 miles per hour). Data is apparently unavailable as to calories expended or weight loss during a sneeze. With little difficulty, one clearly sees the need for the handkerchief industry. In short, sneezing is a most complicated reflex which may be the result of nasal irritation, allergy, infection or chilled body surface. There are even some documented instances of sneezing in response to light (photic sneezes), mental images (specifically erotic thoughts), and other psychosomatic cues. With scientific understanding, one may now move to the cultural, humorous and psychological roles of the sneeze.

As in most life situations, a balance exists between humor and tragedy. The sneeze holds this same strange duality. For instance, the Talmud calls it "A pleasure sent from God." However, Pope Gregory (560-604) questioned the value of this opinion: he believed the sneeze was a beginning symptom of the plague. In an early attempt at primary prevention, he popularized "God bless you" for protection.

In addition, the sneeze may not always leave one with a pleasurable experience. Records attest to the possibility of varying degrees of discomfort as a result of a "simple" sneeze. For instance, one case cites a sudden hearing loss following a sneeze. There are other cases of being visibly fatigued after the violent expiration of air. Taking this a step further, the author, while in clinical training, remembers one professor equating the point between the inspiration and expiration of air as a "near-death" experience. Fortunately, no case was found to illustrate this point.

On the humorous side, there is the poetic case of Ogden Nash's bugler, Douglas MacDougal. This is such a noteworthy example that it stands alone without explanation. It is one of those rare occurrences immortalized in verse which few people are destined to know, to understand and, most importantly for my scientific readers, to replicate. From a writer's perspective, no segue, topic or summary sentence does it justice. It is presented as follows: Apparently times were hard for this bugler. In either a desire to be frugal due to lack of funds or to be tunefully unique, Douglas MacDougal learned how to sneeze in various musical keys, thus saving the price of a bugle. According to most sources, this was one of the few truly successful attempts in history to toot one's own horn.

Finally, there are approximately twelve recorded cases of intractable sneezing. These are simultaneously rare, painful, humorous, incredulous, and perhaps psychologically based. Most people have experienced two, three, even four consecutive sneezes; but few have experienced intractable sneezing continuing for extended periods of time with little relief.

The record is held by an individual who, after recovering from influenza, sneezed 25 times a minute for three consecutive years. With calculator in hand, that equates to a sneeze for every two heartbeats; three sneezes for every two heartbeats; three sneezes per breath; 1,500 per hour; 36,000 each day; 13,400,000 each year. Imagine the potential side effects over the three-year period: chewing food rapidly between sneezes, little participation in public events, numerous dreams about wind, constant fatigue, poor concentration, questionable conversational skills, insomnia, and consecutively frustrated physicians. Though most agree that this person's problem was suggestive and psychosomatic, the exact cause and specific treatment responsible for this miraculous cure is unknown. The patient was finally cured on the 39,420,000th sneeze.

Other cases of intractable sneezing have ranged from three a minute for 33 days to 700 sneezes in 30 minutes. Ages ranged from eleven to forty years old. All cases, fortunately, reported cures.

For those curious as to the cures involved, these most extreme cases were solved variously by drug therapy, antihistamines, desensitization, hypnosis and several forms of psychological treatment — including psychotherapy for one victim's mother.

To summarize, the sneezing process is simply one part of being human. It serves a valuable function, daily activated involuntarily as a defense. For the average person, the sneeze is usually little more than a tickling in the nose and occupies the same place of prominence as other potentially human foibles such as yawning, hiccoughing and snoring.

A sneeze may result from a combination of both physiological and psychological properties. It is likely that nerve receptor sites respond to tangible irritation and perhaps perceived or imagined mental images. Though sneezing can be painful, damage rarely occurs.

A psychological side effect of sneezing is attention. Observers will usually wish one good health and blessings. If consecutive sneezes occur, the novelty brings more positive side effects like understanding laughter and "that once happened to me" stories.

In order to enjoy sneezing as a potential source of satisfac-

tion, to reduce physical discomfort and to minimize the possibility of ostracism, the following rules are offered: 1. Turn
your head and direct the sneeze away from other people's immediate territory; 2. Avoid announcing a sneeze, as they are
easy to spot — a simple "Excuse me" will do; 3. Either carry a
handkerchief to reduce spray or reconsider extending your
hand when the conversation is over; 4. During a sneeze,
remember your train of thought and feel for the interrupted
conversation; 5. Reduce the probability of sneezing, if desired,
by diverting your mental images using the "index finger under
the nose trick"; and 6. Try sneezing with a straight face.

References:
Co, S. "Intractable Sneezing." *The Archives of Neurology*, 1979, *36*, pp. 111-
    112.

Trimble, G.X. "Critique and Cavil... (Sneeze II)." *The Journal of the American
    Medical Association*, 1974, *229*, p.800.

LIGHTEN UP!

Light. It's something we all take for granted; yet most
people (including scientists and other researchers) are in the
dark when it comes to the real facts surrounding the subject.
Not only does light illuminate our surroundings, but it affects
behavior in ways psychologists, sociologists, and physicians are
just now beginning to comprehend.

For example, during the summer months, office and home
responsibilities are rescheduled to include as many outside activities as possible. Picnics in the park, suntans at the beach,
walks by the river, and amusement outings become the order
of the day. We tend to forget the gray days of winter and now
are motivated to enjoy the daylight hours as much as possible.

At this time, magazines and newspapers are full of warnings about the harmful side of light: overexposure, sunburn, heat exhaustion, and the like.

But new research is pointing out that natural light also has positive side effects which are essential for physical and mental health. Unfortunately, few people are able to take advantage of these benefits. To do so would take major modification of traditional routines, both at home and work.

Lack of exposure to natural light is the result of our spending as much as 90 percent of the time inside buildings and vehicles. Glass windows block out the greater part of the light spectrum. Consequently, it has been estimated that 16 hours of artificial lighting provide less physical and emotional benefits than one hour of natural lighting. Traditional inside illumination, provided at home and on the job (the accepted standard is between 50 and 100 footcandles), hardly meets the need nor is it the same as "real" light. It accounts for less than ten percent of the light normally found in the shade of an oak tree on a bright, sunny day. As a result, most of us may not be getting our recommended daily allowance of natural light.

Light has always been a universal sign of beneficence and renewal. In addition to its symbolic value, physicians in ancient Egypt used light as a facilitator of healing. Even as late as the 1900s, various maladies were treated with colored lights. Unfortunately, the approach ultimately became a fad. With that, both the medical and lay communities lost interest in the procedure. Only recently has there been a resurgence of interest and positive research to warrant its study.

Common-sense biology and psychology easily suggest that light has an effect on human beings. Empirical research also supports this premise. To that point, two research areas have emerged that identify specific behavioral responses to lighting: evidence that light can be used medically, and that it directly impacts on human expectations and relations with others.

Light was shown to be an agent of cure in 1903. At that time, Niels R. Finsen of Denmark was awarded the Nobel prize for his pioneering work on the curative properties of light. He investigated how animals respond to sunshine and drew the conclusion that light was beneficial and necessary to the health of an organism.

As a result of his initial investigation, he used light in the treatment of smallpox. He found that scarring was dramatically reduced and that light was quite effective in curing a then-common tubercular skin infection.

However, a more dramatic finding later demonstrated light's curative properties. At a local hospital in Rockford, England in the mid-1950s, a nurse serendipitously found a cure which has since saved the lives of many infants. Sister Ward, the nurse in charge of a newborn unit, was a firm believer in the value of fresh air and sunshine. She routinely took infants out for therapeutic basks in the sun. In one case, an infant was jaundiced and had a condition diagnosed today as hyper-bilirubinemia. (Common in premature infants, this disorder denotes a higher than usual level of bilirubin, a red pigment in bile. Actually, most newborns have some degree of elevated bilirubin with symptomatic yellowing or jaundice.)

Sister Ward had a physician examine the infant in question. He noticed a strange, triangular patch of yellow on the baby's tummy. This patch matched the corner of a blanket which had accidentally fallen across the child while sun-bathing. In other words, the sun had bleached out the jaundice on the rest of the body; the only yellow which remained was that which received no sunlight.

In the area of mental illness, light has also been shown to be an effective agent in the treatment of some forms of depression. As light enters the eye, researchers believe that it somehow stimulates the pineal gland, which plays an important role in a person's adjustment to his or her environment. As the days grow shorter and darker, the pineal gland secretes melatonin.

Researchers believe that there is a link between melatonin and some forms of emotional disorder.

There is a rare form of depression which is common in fall and winter months. This problem, Seasonal Affective Disorder (SAD), is more common as the days begin to grow short. Researchers have hypothesized that as the days change, the depressed person's internal "clock" begins to run behind. To resolve this problem and decrease depression, patients are asked to sit under a very bright light for several hours each day. Full-spectrum lighting is very similar to natural lighting in that it includes ultraviolet and visible parts of the spectrum. After basking under the lights, mood changed, and depression was not as pronounced.

One important lesson which can be taken from this example is the effect of light on reducing jet lag. If light works to reset, synchronize, or entrain the biological clock, it follows that it might be effective in reducing this syndrome. There is evidence that jet lag is alleviated by taking a nice, long walk in the sunshine soon after arrival at a destination. By doing this, the body modifies its old cycle to match the new light/dark hours.

These examples have focused on the internal, more physiological effects of light. But light can also have an effect on more obvious behaviors.

The best way to observe how lighting affects moods is to vary its intensity. In a recent study, 140 blood donors were observed. Half of the participants sat in a brightly lit room with overhead lighting. The rest of the subjects waited in a room lit only by table lamps.

Blood donors who waited under bright lights avoided interaction with others. They sat further apart, read books or magazines, and sat further apart, read books or magazines, and sat with their backs toward the middle of the room. People who waited in the dimly lit room did just the opposite. There was greater interaction, and the donors sat closer together. Chatting to pass the time, they also chose to sit facing the middle of the room with their backs to the wall.

Dim light allows people to feel close to others around them. This would explain why parties and nightclubs traditionally have lower lights. Dim lights during a candlelit dinner help a couple focus on each other and not extraneous stimuli.

Dimly lit rooms with colored lights also affect behavior. This is especially true in casino settings. A British study investigating gambling practices found that those individuals who sat near red lights gambled more by selecting riskier bets.

There's also another curious finding about dim light. When lights are low, people tend to speak softly to each other. In fact, researchers have found that conversations in dimly lit rooms average nine decibels lower than average talk. In dim light, interactions can become more intimate, and conversations are quieter and more deliberate.

If dim lights allow a person to move at a slower pace, do bright lights produce an opposite effect? As a general rule, yes. For instance, as lighting becomes brighter, worker productivity tends to increase. However, there is evidence that bright overhead lights may precipitate boredom, headaches, and eye fatigue.

But the culprit may not be the lighting. Glare is a problem that can bring productivity in any form to a screeching halt. To remedy this problem, experts suggest dimming the lights slightly, changing the work surface to a less reflective material, and varying the angle at which light hits the work area.

There is more to light than meets the eye. Natural light is restorative and needed for both physical and mental health. Additionally, light also impacts on emotions, productivity levels, expectations, and friendships. The study of light and its effect on daily life is still a relatively new area, but preliminary data suggests that it holds great potential for a bright future

References:
Meer, J. The light touch. *Psychology Today,* September, 1985, pp. 60-67.

Shodell, M. The curative light. *Science*, April, 1982, pp. 47-51.

Wurtman, R.J. The effects of light on the human body. *Scientific American*, July, 1975, pp. 68-78.

SOUNDING OFF

Due to advances in computer technology and the ability to create sounds never heard before, neurologists and psychologists are gaining a better understanding of that which stimulates the auditory nerves. And as a result of researchers' ability to manipulate and create sounds, there is a great deal of new evidence demonstrating that sounds and resulting behaviors have both a genetic and learned (or associated) basis.

This means we come into the world "prewired" to respond to certain sounds. But it doesn't stop there. We can then take those sounds, add to them, and continually create a "sound collection" associated with thoughts, feelings, and other behavioral responses.

Because the sense of sound is highly developed at birth, one researcher used infants to demonstrate the genetic link between sounds and behavior.

In a series of psychological studies conducted over a period of years, musical phrases (consisting of three tones) were played to see how infants would respond. Each of the three musical tones was created by computer. Though the order of the tones varied, the same three notes were repeated over and over. After those were established, the researcher inserted stray notes.

In order for the infants to respond to the stray notes, each child had to recognize or remember which notes were in the original sequence. The researchers did not know if the infants would remember all notes, one set of notes, or none.

What they found was surprising. The infants could only remember three notes. Those notes were C, E, and G. If you have a musical background, you understand the significance of the finding. They are the ones most typically found in Western melodies. Other researchers have pointed out that this finding concerning genetic wiring doesn't vary from culture to culture, and may be the neurological bottom line which allows us to process music and other sounds.

To further elaborate and lend credence to this idea, anthropologists point out that musical sounds share certain elements on a cross-cultural basis. These standard findings include pitches separated by definable intervals, musical scales from five to seven notes, and scales arranged in octaves.

There is more evidence that sounds link us genetically to the past. If you have ever heard the shriek of chalk or fingernails scraping across a blackboard, or the squeal of metal against stone during honing, then you have experienced this phenomenon firsthand.

Where do these spine-tingling aversions to certain sounds come from? Unfortunately, no one knows for sure. However, very few people can hear these sounds without cringing. It is believed that the reason behind the response lies in our prehistoric roots.

To explain, a group of researchers taped a scraping sound (garden fork across a slate surface) and fed the recording into a computer. Then, using a process called "digital filtering," selected frequencies were removed from the original sound. Participants in the study listened to the original and filtered versions, rating them for unpleasantness.

They found that filtered versions had differing impact when

compared to the original squeal. When the shrill, higher frequencies were removed, people found them just as unpleasant as the original. However, when the lower frequencies were removed, participants did not find the version objectionable. In fact, the sound was rather tame. All alone, the high frequencies sounded pleasingly odd.

Even with this new information, the researchers failed to find out why some scraping sounds will send chills up and down our spines.

The answer came when they compared the scraping sound wave with that of some naturally occurring sounds. The scraping sound (like the squeal of chalk) is remarkably similar to the warning cries of wild monkeys. The aversion response may be a vestigial reflex courtesy of our primate ancestors.

In addition to genetic evidence, there is also the learned or associated link between sounds and human behavior. In fact, one researcher has estimated that 70 percent of our responses to sound comes from associations − pairing a sound with an event. Over time, certain sounds become associated with significant events like dating, marriage, or graduation.

One obvious example of pairing sound with behavior is well known to moviegoers. Take John Williams' disturbing score for *Jaws*. Jagged, insistent rhythms provoked tension, dread, and fear. Similarly, Williams' score for *Star Wars* used a strong melodious leitmotif for each character. The pairing of sound with action was so strong that when you left the theater and heard either the music from *Jaws* or *Star Wars*, you were immediately transported back to the movie. The same happens in everyday life, even if you don't realize it.

It's a matter of three simple steps. First, a sound is heard. Second, an individual relates the sound to past experiences, or creates new mental engrams or pictures to represent what is heard. Finally, a personalized response (thought, feeling, or behavior) emerges. That's why some sounds evoke pleasant memories, feelings, thoughts, and behaviors — and others tend to remind us of past pain, embarrassment, and fear.

In addition, there are a great many facets which determine how sound affects behavior. These include loudness, pitch, frequency, timbre, and others. But the key lies within the human perception or amalgamation of these facets into one identified sound. How we individually process and associate specific sounds with past or current learning determines what behaviors will follow. In other words, sounds can facilitate certain actions or abilities, and inhibit others.

It has been shown that certain sounds can facilitate memory, reduce pain, and evoke feelings.

In the area of memory, 36 undergraduates were taught a list of 40 common, everyday words while listening to an audiotape of either a Mozart concerto or a jazz instrumental. Other students learned the same list, with no musical background. Two days after the initial learning session, the experimenters measured the participants' recall.

Based on this experimental design, it would appear that the researchers were trying to find out which music better facilitated memory. Mozart or jazz? The researchers did not find that classical was "better" than jazz, but achieved a more practical finding.

Better memory was the result of hearing music while learning the material, and then rehearing the *same* music again two days later when asked to recall the words. If you heard classical music in session one, hearing the same Mozart concerto two days later assisted your memory. The students did not test as well if they heard classical first and jazz second. Those who learned in silence did as well with either a Mozart, jazz, or silent background. In this experiment, a quiet environment was of small benefit in recall, but the same sounds in both session one and two actively cued memory.

For example, say you are studying for a test. Study consistently with the same type of music, then, at exam time, answer the test questions while listening to a cassette recording of the same music. In an academic setting, teachers may not go along with this, because answers can also be recorded. So, for maximum benefits, vary the settings where you study and learn the initial material; then, a silent testing room will not be a shock.

The ramifications of this study go far beyond the classroom. Working on the same project over a period of time? Use the same type of music as a mental aid. The same sounds get you in the mood, because they are associated with work and facilitate your memory. Planning a television advertising campaign? If the first commercial is a success, make sure the follow-up ones use the same music.

Moreover, consistent sounds may also reduce stress. In a recent study, migraine sufferers were given relaxation training while listening to music. They imagined tranquil, peaceful scenes while listening to a medley of popular songs. Only ten, 30- minute sessions over a five-week period were necessary to associate relaxation with music.

To determine training effectiveness, participants kept a diary of the number, intensity, and duration of each headache during training. Additionally, a weekly diary was maintained at monthly and yearly intervals. After training, they used the same music paired with relaxation. As a result, the headache sufferers had only one-sixth as many migraines as they had before.

It is not known why musical sounds aid relaxation and reduce the number of headaches. What is known is that certain musical sounds tend to release endorphins, the body's natural painkillers. This same type finding is being replicated in delivery rooms, as expectant mothers displayed fewer pain responses when music accompanied labor. Additionally, music and other sound therapy represents a new frontier in working with autistic children. Sounds can soothe, reduce pain, evoke feelings, and prompt physiological changes.

Newborns seem to respond physiologically to sounds. Babies (and adults, too) will show fluctuations in heart rates as a result of hearing certain sounds. When an infant or adult pays close attention to any sound, heart rate decreases; when emotions take over, the rate rises to its normal or higher level. Older children display more overt emotional reactions.

Without prompting, young children will point to drawings or happy faces when listening to high-pitched, up-tempo sounds. Conversely, when the music is lower pitched, children more readily point to sad faces. Some researchers think that children learn to respond this way based on their listening to nursery rhymes, lullabies, and even a parent's tone of voice. Other researchers think that the genetic link is where it all starts.

There is a new world of research focusing on how and why sounds influence us the way they do. In medicine, sound waves may represent a break-through in healing. In the field of mental health, sounds are providing the common denominator necessary to our better understanding of illness. In entertainment, computers are challenging us with sounds never heard before. Finally, within our own lives, sounds are more than a means of communication. They are a link to our past

References:
Blake, R. Primal screech. *Psychology Today*, 1986, *20*, p. 68.

Chance, P. Music hath charms to soothe a throbbing head. *Psychology Today*, 1987, *21*, p. 14.

Hanswer, S., Larson, S., & O'Connell, A. Music therapy-assisted labor: Effects on relaxation of expectant mothers. *Birth Psychology Bulletin*, 1983, *4*, pp. 2-13.

Meer, J. A sound memory. *Psychology Today*, 1986, *20,* p. 76.

Monmaney, T. Key notes on the mind. *Omni,* 1987, *9*, p. 45ff.

Morrongiello, B., & Clifton, R. Effects of sound frequency on behavioral and cardiac orienting in newborn and five-month-old infants. *Journal of Experimental Child Psychology*, 1984, *38*, pp. 429-446.

EXPOSING THE YAWN

Don't try to deny it; everyone does it. The living world yawns. Day-old infants do it. Your dog and cat can't keep a straight face. Alligators wake up doing it. And, of course, psychologists have found a way to chemically stimulate those "fun-loving" white rats. As a result, they (the rats, not the psychologists) have learned to yawn on electrical cue. So, with this brief introduction, here begins an expose of the yawn.

If you don't understand the "what" and the "why" behind the yawn, you're in good company. The yawn is one of those human attributes (right up there with dimples, stomach "butterflies," goose flesh, and double-jointedness) that people talk about, but about which little scientific study is thought necessary. Think about it: very few (if any) people study yawns for a living. It would, however, be an inflation-proof industry.

The yawn held practical value for Hippocrates, the father of medicine. This 5th-century B.C. physician concluded that intense or prolonged yawning was a proof-positive symptom of an impending fever. He was incorrect. In fact, there is little evidence that the yawn has any diagnostic significance.

There is a strange medical twist, however. Persons with acute illnesses yawn less when their condition remains serious. In other words, yawning may be a sign of convalescence. Furthermore, psychotic persons (those individuals who are out of touch with reality) rarely yawn. There is no explanation for that little piece of trivia.

History documents few attempts between the 5th century

B.C. and modern times to explain the yawn. Charles Darwin observed that baboons reveal hostility by yawning. He suggested that humans may do the same. There is no evidence to support this supposition.

One modern scientific achievement has been to "rename" the yawn. As indicative of most high-technology labels and other scientific nomenclature, the new term has more than three syllables and, on the surface, looks as if it has nothing to do with yawning. Moreover, if you saw this term in your medical record, you would probably conclude that you had some dread disease.

To yawn is to "oscitate." If you stretch while yawning, you are said to "pandiculate."

Continuing with other bizarre trivia, the most astounding case of uncontrollable yawning — oscitation, rather — was a case documented in 1888. As reported, a 15-year- old female yawned continuously for five successive weeks. Fortunately, the unnamed treatment was ultimately successful. This may be the closest that any human has come to boring herself to death.

However, it is impossible to conclude that this woman yawned out of boredom. (In fact, there was a lot going on in 1888!) Boredom is not necessarily the cause of yawning. For instance, there's the following example.

Imagine a candlelight, romantic dinner for two. You and your date are enjoying each other's company. It's a perfect evening. All of a sudden and for no apparent reason, your date yawns. You can hardly believe your eyes and ears. You are mortified, hurt, angry and confused. How could your date find you, of all people, boring?

Boredom was probably *not* the case. It could easily be any one of the following reasons. Maybe the service was slow, and hunger was the culprit. Perhaps she had a hard day at work, and fatigue prompted the yawn. Another explanation could be indigestion. Even poor ventilation may trigger an involuntary gaping. Perhaps she saw someone else yawn, and the copycat instinct took over. Or if Darwin was correct, you would be wise to find out what you did wrong and promptly apologize.

In addition, if this is your first date, then a yawn may be a signal of a person's struggle to be attentive or to adapt to a new situation. To further explain, people will upon occasion yawn when leaving a movie, though the movie was not boring. Some research supports the fact that a yawn is necessary to readapt. As you leave the movie theatre, you yawn to readjust to reality; and in the morning, you yawn to adjust to awakening.

What is a yawn? Here's the technical data.

A yawn is a complex, automatic, physiological experience whereby the lungs fully expand, the heart generates greater activity, and the blood receives more oxygen. The yawn begins with an involuntary spasm of the muscles of mastication and swallowing. It ends quietly with a sigh.

A yawn is a long, deep, involuntary intake of air, accompanied by an unusual expansion of the chest, gaping of the mouth, and elevation of the shoulders. You cannot subdue a yawn once it starts. If you try, everything continues to happen, your mouth wrinkles — making the yawn more conspicuous than it originally was.

Now, the next question is "Why do we yawn?" When you are exhausted, drowsy or fatigued, your breathing becomes shallow. Your rate of respiration slows down. Under regular operating conditions, you will inhale and exhale approximately 12 to 24 times a minute. This lung work nets your body nine to 12 pints of air. That expands mathematically (using 12 breaths a minute) to 720 breaths an hour; 17,280 breaths daily; 6,307,200 yearly. And assuming you live to be 65 years of age, you have mastered the art of breathing with the number of breaths reaching exponential proportions. That means that the total number goes off the edge of your calculator.

If your breathing rate drops to seven or eight times per

minute for an extended period of time and your activity level does not decrease, you are depriving your body of oxygen. Carbon dioxide, which under normal conditions would be exhaled, is now increasing in the body. Simply put, as you breathe, you inhale oxygen and exhale carbon dioxide. It's actually the carbon dioxide in the blood stream which returns the respiration rate to its regular, normal level.

Nerve cells, located in the respiratory center of the brain (in the brain stem just above the spinal cord), are most sensitive to the amount of carbon dioxide in the body. When there is too much of it, the center signals the lungs to breathe deeper and faster. At the same time, the autonomic nervous system forwards a message to the facial muscles around the jaw. Your muscles now contract, forcing you to yawn and to take an extra deep breath. As a result, you take in an extra dose of oxygen and cleanse your system of excessive carbon dioxide. You'll probably notice that you feel more relaxed and refreshed after yawning. This results not only from extra oxygen, but improved circulation when neck, chest and other muscles stretch and contract. A yawn is a boost to the body.

What about the copycat yawn? Psychologists are not exactly sure why one person's yawning will trigger that same response in you. Suffice it to say, professors are well aware of "yawning class syndrome." Actually, if you look around right now, you will probably see more yawns than usual. That's not because this flight or article is boring, but because a yawning thought has been planted. Don't be surprised if you yawn before you finish reading.

Can you yawn a bona fide yawn by telling yourself to yawn? Probably not; fake yawns don't look like the real thing no matter how much you try. However, if you really want to try to induce one, the following procedure may be helpful.

Strive for the following setting: a warm, dry, not well-ventilated room. Next, role play or go through the motions of yawning several times. As you do this, lower your eyelids, roll the eyeballs up slightly, and then lift the eyelids. Chances are that you didn't yawn the first time; however, if you try it enough times, you will probably yawn out of desperation. Trust your body; you'll yawn when you need to.

There is also some evidence to support the fact that a yawn may be an expression of tension. Therefore, a yawn would be the body's way of helping you resolve and reduce stress. There is little doubt that a yawn, although unplanned and uncontrollable, can actually be quite pleasurable.

One additional point for the airline traveler: a yawn has an interesting side-effect. Frequent travelers are well aware of the effects of pressurized cabins. As a result, some chew gum to help equalize inner-ear pressure, and others make strange faces so "their ears will pop." A stretching yawn also helps to equalize pressure in your ears. As a result, discomfort is minimized.

Finally, there is the psychology of yawning. Let's say that you don't want to be bothered, but you don't have the courage to tell folks to leave you alone. All you have to do is yawn, turn your head and smack your lips a few times. They will get the hint that you are "so tired," "worked so hard," and, as a result, treat you like a "babe in a cradle." Your yawn is a signal to the entire world to "bug off." Now you can settle in and do what you want to do without interference.

There's no need to stifle a yawn. Express yourself; be creative. For the sake of delicacy, please cover your mouth as you yawn, and an "excuse me" is in order. But don't worry about yawning, because one thing's for sure: yawn and the world yawns with you... even if they don't want to.

References:
Abarbanel, A. What's in a yawn? *Today's Health*, 1964, *42*, p. 30.

Rosen, M. Those funny things your body does. *Family Health*, 1976, *8*, p. 76.

THE SOUNDS OF SLEEP

He stretched, following eight hours of sound sleep, rolled over and smiled at his wife.

As he said, "Good morning," he noticed her eyes were red and swollen, her bed clothes were excessively wrinkled and she was not smiling.

"You kept me awake all night," she retorted, "because you *snored* again!" Then, she asked for a divorce.

Other sleep sounds — sighing, murmuring and talking — don't have the potential to irritate or to fascinate as a sonorous snore. As an observer of human behavior, here's an in-depth look at grandma's wheeze and grandpa's freight-train rumble.

Researchers do not know why people snore. Moreover, why one person snores on some nights and not on others, or at different times in a single night is equally a mystery. One thing is for sure, snoring is involuntary and stops as soon as you wake up. As a result of this paradox, one is unable to hear oneself perform.

The discordant notes of snoring are maximized when the sleeper is lying on his back with the head sagging on the chest. This produces a bending of the trachea, compressing the respiratory tube. As a result, there is an obstruction of air passage. To signal this blockage, a man-made flute is created, producing sounds with a distinctively individual pitch and varied intensity. In fact, one possible side effect of snoring is damage to the hearing mechanism, which is not unusual given a snore's potential volume.

The loudest snore recorded by Guinness is 69 decibels. Scientists have reported the snore's noise level (measured approximately five feet from the sleeper) to be between 60 and 80 decibels. For frame of reference, a normal conversation ranges from 50 to 70 decibels; and a New York subway averages around 115 decibels.

Many people confuse "snorts" with snoring. These are as different as your nose and mouth. To explain, breathing through the nose does not produce snoring; rather, the sounds which result are snorts or a series of snorts. These preliminary sounds mark the first stage; the second, or the true snore, results when the sleeper opens his mouth. According to physiologists, relaxation of general muscle tone runs parallel to the depth or intensity of sleep. As a result, the tongue and jaw muscles relax and fall back simply because of their weight. Mouth breathing and snoring follow.

Statistics inform that 45 percent of normal subjects occasionally snore and 25 percent are habitual snorers. For children, snoring is often associated with enlarged tonsils and adenoids. As one grows older, particularly men, snoring becomes frequent. Finally, snoring is three times more common in obese individuals.

Animals appear to be protected from the snoring phenomena. Naturalists inform that animals sleep in one of two positions: ventral (belly-side) or side. As a result, their lower jaws are sustained, preventing them from falling back. It would appear that snoring is exclusively human, although some pet-owners might disagree.

In addition to the social stigma, snoring, which is not considered a natural process, may have some definite damaging effects. For instance, complaints of dry mouth and sore throat are common. Other reported problems include fatigue/exhaustion as a result of nightly snoring, severe headaches, diseases of teeth and gums, tonsillitis, sinusitis, laryngitis, bronchitis and serious damage to the hearing mechanism (remember the pneumatic drill and imagine listening to oneself snore for eight hours).

Although the cause of snoring is unknown, treatments are

common. In fact, more than 300 devices to stop snoring have been registered with the U.S. Patent Office. These include sewing squeakers into the back of nightwear, lashing wrists to the sides of bed, and, of course, chin straps to keep the mouth shut.

One of the most interesting treatments for snoring was described by Dugas in 1852. He suggested that snoring could be prevented by removing the uvula (the small, fleshy appendage hanging from the middle of the soft palate above the back of the tongue). This procedure was abandoned because it did not work. The patients snored more loudly.

A 100-percent cure for snoring is to stop sleeping. The longest period recorded without sleep is 440 hours (18 days and 8 hours). However, a true snoring success story was reported recently in *El Familiar* (September, 1980). The case documents a 57-year-old woman who hasn't slept in over thirty years. The sleeplessness began in 1943 while she was watching a religious procession. She yawned and felt a sudden pain. As a result, sleeplessness followed. Consecutively frustrated physicians have finally agreed that the sleep section of her brain appears to be permanently impaired. Insomnia is a cure for snoring.

In a recent issue of the *Journal of the American Medical Association* (October, 1980), a "Letter to the Editor" suggested that individuals who have snoring problems use a cervical collar at bedtime. Such a collar is the same kind used to treat a sprained neck. According to the author, the collar will "keep the chin elevated and prevent the flexing of the trachea that causes the compression and results in the harsh emitted sound." Be sure to consult your physician, but this idea may hold some promise.

Much has been written about the snorer, but the "snoree" has been ignored. The snorer does not realize what is going on, because he is able to sleep through it. However, snorees, who must endure the noise, are the victims of an infinite psychological cycle, and probably don't realize it. They are consumed with the thought that they "can't get to sleep because *snorers* are keeping them awake." As a result, a futile attempt at taking actions begins. The more they plot strategies to get to sleep, the more slowly sleep comes. As each strategy fails, the cycle continues.

Techniques to reduce the snorer's blasts usually progress in this order: 1. Wake snorer, who within minutes (before you have a chance to get to sleep) starts snoring again; 2. pillow and covers over head, which are uncomfortable and only partially reduce the noise; 3. ear plugs, which are a problem should an emergency arise in the home; 4. a scientific white-noise generator (an electric device which simulates "fan-sounding" tones and covers other noises) which partially obliterates snoring; 5. separate bedrooms, and 6. as a last resort, another house. Each of these procedures is only partially effective, because none of them reduces anger, which is often directed at the snorer.

The anger is a direct result of "How dare you do this to me." In situations where one person snores and the mate does not, bedtime becomes a race. A race of "I'll try to get to sleep before my snoring partner, and then I'll have a good night's rest."

If the snoree gets to sleep first, it is an effective aid to combating snoring. However, if the snorer gets to sleep first... problems. Chances are, the more you try to race, the longer you will stay awake and the more the snoring will irritate you. As you strive to fall asleep first, you indirectly keep yourself awake. Put another way, your constant desire to get to sleep first provides reminders of all past evenings when your sleep was disturbed. If you lose the race, your anger, because you feel cheated, keeps you awake.

To resolve the snoring problem, encourage your partner to keep his mouth shut. In fact, that's pretty good advice for most situations. Snuggling a pillow tightly under or next to your partner may help keep him on his side or stomach. A pillow under the chin may also be effective. However, when the support moves, a chronic snorer will resume old behaviors.

Patience is important, but good sleep behavior is essential for the snorer and partner. It is necessary, physiologically and psychologically, that both cultivate sound sleep behaviors which guarantee daily rest. Sleep interruption is counter-productive to all involved.

Snoring is perfectly human, but sometimes it is impossible to ig- snore.

References:

Seifert, P., & Bay, E. Snoring. *Southern Medical Journal*, 1980, *73*, pp. 1035-1037.

Zwillich, C. The clinical significance of snoring. *Archives of Internal Medicine*, 1979, *139*, p. 24.

MAKE 'EM LAUGH

Let's take a good look at laughter. Now, most people tend to include it in the same category with yawning, sneezing, "goose- pimples," "stomach butterflies" and double jointedness. But a good belly laugh just doesn't belong in the same category. To laugh, something has to be funny; and goosepimples (and the above list) just don't qualify — and that's no joke.

The scientific name for laughter is "risus." That name, however, doesn't seem to be as suitably descriptive as the everyday vernacular. For instance, take "belly laugh" — not phonetically very delicate, but you can picture it. Or "gullible giggle," which evokes a totally different picture. Or a "giant guffawer." The point here is well taken — the name, "risus," and the ensuing behavior don't quite fit.

Simply put, a good case of the giggles is good for you. It has no serious side effects (unless you fall out of your chair laughing), and it will keep the doctors away with as much efficiency, if not more, than apples or vitamins.

Laughter simultaneously exercises the physical and mental systems. Physiologically, for instance, a good guffaw exercises the lungs and invigorates the circulatory system. Strong laughter also prompts complete action of the diaphragm. When this happens, the entire cardiovascular system is stimulated and the oxygen level is increased in the blood.

So, you see, laughter is a type of internal jogging. Here's what it looks like from the inside out when your best friend says, "You want to hear a joke?"

Within the few opening seconds of the joke, muscle tension begins to increase in anticipation of the funny climax. You may even "suffer" a giggle or a smile — just with the belief alone that the joke will make you laugh. Finally, just what you wanted did in fact happen — it was a funny joke after all. As you laugh, your entire body gets a super workout. Your thorax (chest), abdomen, and face receive a vigorous overhaul. When an individual really "breaks up," the result is convulsive laughter, the kind you can't stop even if you want to — even the legs and arms get involved.

You may never have thought about muscle tension increasing in anticipation of a good laugh. But to prove the point, think back to the last time a friend's joke wasn't funny. The tenseness was there to enjoy a laugh, but you were "let down." The disappointment is worse, because both your friend and your body set you up.

Sometimes laughter appears to have a "mind of its own." It's not difficult for you to remember situations when, no matter how hard you tried, you couldn't stop laughing. These instances usually come in quiet situations in a person's life, like in a library or at a serious meeting. As one of the rites of passage, this problem invariably occurs in the life of the third-grader. As the child sits there trying to control his or her giggles, the teacher is likely to respond with, "If it's so funny, why don't you tell the entire class?" As you probably learned if that happened to you, sometimes discretion is the better part of valor.

Laughter may indirectly aid in decreasing pain in inflammatory conditions associated with such physical problems as arthritis, for instance. Evidence is beginning to suggest that laughter sends a message to the brain requiring that it produce more "alertness hormones" (the catecholamines). The release of this alertness chemical then stimulates secretions of the body's own pain killers (endorphins), and the perception of pain decreases. The bottom line is that laughter may be a pain killer. An increase in catecholamines has been linked to decreases in inflammation.

There is also evidence that laughter is one method the body employs to relax. When you laugh heartily and the humorous spasm stops, your pulse rate drops below normal, and skeletal muscles become deeply relaxed. The body is revitalized.

The relaxation response has been found to last approximately 45 minutes after the last "ha." The greater the intensity of laughter, the larger the decrease in tension and the more long-lasting the effect. Laughter allows the muscles to go limp, and is an effective agent for reducing stress.

Just where did laughter come from? Laughter — and the debate — have been around for ages. Believe it or not, paintings over 5,000 years ago in Egyptian tombs depict slapstick humor. Some researchers believe, and there is some supporting evidence, that laughter evolved much as our ability to think did. You see, laughter is the result of internal stimulation. Therefore, if you can't think, you can't laugh.

The best way to explain this is to look at the differences between kiddie and adult humor. Kids love riddles, but adults don't usually think that riddles are quite so funny. The reason simply lies in the differences between child and adult thinking. Youngsters are beginning to tackle and to master the use of words. As their ability to use language increases, so does their ability to manipulate language. When this happens, they have the potential to tickle themselves (using language) from the inside out. Kids freely share what tickled them, hoping it will tickle you.

Puns, on the other hand, are generally hilarious to adults, but kids sort of look at you funny (no pun intended). Puns are much more laughable to adults (especially to the one who created it) than they are to children. The adult brain is capable of understanding and creating sophisticated levels of humor; the child's brain is just beginning to master the task. In other words, if you think like an adult, it takes more to make you laugh.

It is with much regret that as one grows older, the ability to produce a laugh becomes more difficult. This changes slightly as one reaches his or her 70s and 80s. As you approach later life, the world tends to be considerably more laughable.

Sages have discussed the question of "why do we laugh?" for years. Psychologists have only studied it since 1928, but what was said then is still laughably revered today. Most agree that laughter originally emerged as a form of communication. For instance, in a tense situation when there has been impending danger or pain, laughter is the signal that all is well. This is certainly true today, as ofttimes someone will crack a joke to ease a tenseness in the air. This is why seemingly innocuous lines which follow "chilling" scenes in movies will always produce laughter. It is a psychological release, and signals "all is normal."

Certain situations are believed to elicit laughter. It is readily heard when there has been a personal triumph or victory. This was certainly the case in *Rocky I, II*, and *III* and will continue to follow if additional films are created. No one likes a sad Rocky. Moreover, political campaigns which are victorious are filled with laughter; the defeated are generally not even smiling.

A surprise or unexpected turn of events will also elicit laughter. This is particularly true if there is a feeling of superiority surrounding the surprise. That's why a practical joke is so funny (provided you're not the brunt of it). It has the element of surprise and an air of "I got you." An unexpected reward has both of these elements.

Tickling will produce laughter, especially in children. No one has any idea how tickling produces laughter — it just does. Don't try and understand it, just enjoy it, especially because it takes two people to tickle.

A funny story causes laughter. The reason it's funny is because the twists and turns of the joke or story build up tension in the listener. Then suddenly, there's an unexpected turn of events, and the tension is released through laughter.

Laughter is aroused in incongruous situations. For instance, imagine you are being interviewed by an individual who is extremely prim and proper. While speaking, he or she leans back in the chair. This would normally be routine; but this time, the "big boss" leans too far back, and the chair overturns. Now, this dignified person peers at you from knee-view while regaining some semblance of decorum. It is a fantasy come true; you lose it in laughter. Of course, you respectfully try to hide your laugh. Flat on his or her face or not, the boss still has the power. This is why the old slapstick "dignified person slipping on the banana" always receives a rousing laugh.

Some people laugh involuntarily to hide shyness or embarrassment. This is the "nervous laugh." This laugh, always easy to spot, doesn't sound like the real thing and is designed to divert one's attention from an uncomfortable situation. Sometimes it works, and sometimes it just shows how shy some people are.

Finally (and fortunately), laughter is positively associated with a sense of well being, good health and social safety. This is psychological jargon for "sad people don't laugh." It's tough when you're depressed to find anything funny at all. Therefore, your amount of laughter is directly related to how much positive regard you have for yourself, and the level with which you feel safe in the world around you.

To illustrate this, there is also some research evidence which suggests that positive things are much easier to remember when laughing or smiling. The converse of that is also true: it is very difficult to remember details of negative events when smiling.

In a recent study, students were asked to read distressing newspaper articles and the "funnies," or comics. At the end of their readings, students were asked to recall the material while frowning, and then smiling. Sad material was more easily remembered while frowning; less distressing material was more easily recalled while smiling. The moral here is to grin while reading the newspaper or watching the news. You won't remember as much!

Yes, the world is less difficult to bear with a smile on your face. The moral to the story is to take the time to enjoy a good laugh. Simply put, if you take the world seriously, you're probably the only one who will. As Will Rogers put it, "We are all here for a spell, get all the good laughs you can."

References:
Hayworth, D. The social origin and function of laughter. *Psychological Review*, 1928, *35*, pp. 367-384.

Jason, K. Smile power. *Omni*, 1984, *6*, p. 37.

Peter, L.J., & Dana, B. *The Laughter Prescription*, New York: Ballantine Books, 1982.

What's the sense of humor. *Science Digest*, 1984, *90*, p. 76.

SOUTHPAW STIGMA

Just because "left" isn't "right" doesn't mean it's wrong. Yet, there's a stigma grown up around "left" — left-handed jokes, left behind, left over, left out, in left field.

As a group, lefties are really alright. After all, if the right-handed majority had been forced to deal with fearful parents, overzealous if well-meaning teachers, and even some pediatricians (all three who constantly insisted you be "other" handed), chances are you'd be a bit edgy, stubborn, and non-conformist, too.

Lefties in our society have a lot to deal with. They are governed by both written and unwritten "bills of rights." Even the vocabulary works against them. For instance, there's no fair shake in an allegedly neutral word like "ambidextrous," which translates literally as being "right-handed on both sides." (Certainly, a one-sided view.)

But left is a negative in several languages. Australians occasionally call left-handed folks "mollydookers," which means "woman-handed." *Gauche* is French for left; "sinister" derives from Latin; *mancino* means deceitful in Italian; *linkisch* implies awkwardness in German; *na levo* means sneaky in Russian; and *zurdo* is Spanish for "malicious." All of these are, at best, left-handed "compliments" to a person who is not right-handed.

Only the Greeks have a good word for the left-handed: *aristera*, which translates as "those fit to govern." To prove the point, left-handed leaders include Tiberius, Alexander the Great, Queen Victoria, and among presidents of the United States, Harry S. Truman, James Garfield and Gerald Ford.

Left-handedness bears the brunt of many superstitions and myths. Some researchers contend that left-handers are brain-damaged, as a result of oxygen deficiencies at birth; predisposed to be alcoholics or suicidal; prone to reading disabilities; better (or worse) in athletics; and have "different" ears for music. But overall, such myths just don't hold up under scientific scrutiny.

The question remains: Why is it sinister to be left-handed? Have we always been a right-handed species? There are archaeologists and cultural anthropologists who argue that Stone Age man was 50% sinistral (left-handed) and 50% dextral (right-handed). The educated guess, however, supports an assertion that the advent of tools and the uniformity of their design indirectly created preference for the right.

Another reason why a negative bias toward left-handedness has emerged was theorized by Carl Sagan in his book, *Dragons of Eden*. He suggested that early man used the left hand for intimate, hygienic purposes and the right for more "civilized" behaviors, like writing and drawing. That would explain why one shakes right hands and embraces others to the right. Concerning cultural conventions, and giving credence to that theory, Hindus use their right hands to touch their bodies above the waist, while the left is used to touch below.

The real cause of handedness is not known. Although mankind has a preference for the right, left-handedness persists. In fact, man appears to be the only creature with any "hand" preference at all. Scientists, naturally, want to know why.

As a result, there is a great deal of research today focused on the relationship between handedness and the two hemispheres of the brain. Brain halves may look similar, but their specialties are unique, according to this research.

The left hemisphere thinks linearly, sequentially, and uses numbers and words. The right, for the majority of us, is concerned with spatial relationships, music, art, and does not use language as we know it.

Remember from introductory psychology how the left hemisphere governs the right motor side of the body, and vice versa? If that is the case, then left-handed people (10% of the population) may be the only ones in their "right" minds.

However, neither left-handedness nor brain-hemisphere dominance is quite so simple. Just like righties, about 60% (a conservative estimate) of lefties have their language centers in the left side of their brains. To date, a really precise location for handedness has not been found; and perhaps left-handedness is just a genetic diversity like gender or eye color, and equally natural.

What about the rumor that left-handers are more creative than right-handers? It may be true. After all, Cole Porter, Michelangelo, Paul McCartney, Rex Harrison, Judy Garland, Leonardo da Vinci, Pablo Picasso and Lewis Carroll begin an impressive list of left-handed creators.

To further illustrate the point, one art teacher/researcher was dismayed by her class' artistic progress. Impulsively and intuitively (a right-hemisphere function), the instructor ordered all her students to switch and use their left hands. The result, according to the teacher's perception, was "more creative" art. So, why not paint with both hands? After all, you play the piano with both.

What about the myth that left-handed athletes have an edge over right-handed players? Although the final score is not in, there are some impressive statistics. To wit, 39 out of 82 batters in baseball's Hall of Fame (as of 1980) were left-handed (four additional ones were switch-hitters), and eleven out of 39 pitchers were southpaws. There may even be some truth that sinistral tennis players (notably Jimmy Connors, John McEnroe and Guillermo Vilas) put a different twist on the ball.

Other athletic lefties include Babe Ruth and Sandy Koufax (baseball), Bill Walton (basketball), Ken Stabler (football), and Mark Spitz (swimming).

Lefties are not so fortunate in polo, however. In fact, one source cited a polo rule which eliminates left-handed players because they are alleged to be dangerous to right-handed players. It's probably all a matter of how you sit the horse.

It seems appropriate to address left-handedness and reading disorders, too. There is a theory which relates sinistrality and dyslexia (an imprecise, almost generic term used to indicate a variety of reading, writing and learning disorders). However, the supporting data are not conclusive and have likely been overinterpreted.

Worthy of mention is Nelson Rockefeller's dyslexic battle which was reported in his obituary in *The New York Times*. According to *The Times*, he had a tendency to read backwards (from right to left), supposedly due to his father's untiring efforts to change young Nelson from left- to right-handed. The story goes that during dinner time, the senior Rockefeller placed a rubber band around his son's wrist, tied a long string to it, and would jerk the string, thus snapping the rubber band, whenever young Nelson would use his left hand. From a psychological vantage, this early attempt at behavior modification is *not* recommended.

There is some evidence (also inconclusive) that left-handedness runs in families, but in no identifiable pattern. Here are the data: 1. 50% of the offspring of two left-handed parents were righties; and 2. 84% of lefties had two right-handed parents. In short, no one knows why a person becomes left-handed.

Do psychologists have a good definition for left-handedness? Is there a clear understanding of why people are left-handed as opposed to right-handed? Are left-handed people significantly different from others? Do parents need to worry and try to change their children's handedness? No, no, no, and NO, respectively.

It is probably not a bad idea, then, to try to put a stop to the stigma that surrounds southpaws and to conclude that those who are other than right-handed be left alone!

References:

Carter-Saltzman, L. Biological and Sociocultural effects of handedness: Comparisons between biological and adoptive families. *Science,* 1980, *209*, pp. 1263-1265.

Chipkin, H. The truth about lefties. *Family Health*, 1979, *11,* p. 38ff.

Fincher, J. Is it sinister to be left-handed? *Reader's Digest,* 1979, *114*, pp. 151-154.

Left-handedness is not a birth defect, experts say. *Today's Child*, February, 1982, p. 3.

MAKING (BODY) SENSE

There's no doubt about it. Your body makes good sense out of its senses. In fact, your senses are so organized that you don't even think about them. But, if for some reason they stopped working — well, it would be impossible to make sense out of that.

Take a quick test and name the body's senses. Most people stop after they have listed seeing, smelling, tasting, hearing and touching. Be warned: you failed the test if you only listed these basic five. There are others, but first a review.

How powerful is your vision? Actually, you can see a candle flame from a distance of 30 miles (assuming it's a very clear and very dark night). Vision is usually the dominant sense and certainly our window to the world. Approximately 70 percent of the information that reaches the brain comes from vision. To prove how vision dominates, finger-trace the number two on your forehead; it will "feel" backwards. Yet, if you trace the number two on the back of your head, it will feel "normal," even though it's actually "backwards." This is because your eyes, which face forward, dominate the senses.

It would be possible to survive without the chemical senses of smell (olfaction) and taste (gustation). However, lower animals would be at a definite disadvantage. For them, smell reveals the presence of predators, and taste (working in conjunction with smell) helps determine edible food. In fact, dogs have seven times as much brain area devoted to smell as humans do. Although an animal's sense of smell is much more acute than that of a typical human, you can still manage to smell one drop of perfume permeating throughout a small house.

For humans, smell and taste take on new meaning at 5 p.m. At that point in the day, these two senses are at their most sensitive. Obviously, this is a dangerous time for weight-watchers. Starve off until 8 p.m., when the day's intake of food and water has been stored, and body weight peaks. Furthermore, never tip the scales at 8 p.m., or you'll be sorry.

You have four primary taste qualities, or sensations. You are most sensitive to bitter and sour, less sensitive to salt, and least to sweet. This order has aided survival as man foraged for food. Your sense of taste is so well developed that you can taste one teaspoon of sugar dissolved in two gallons of water. One problem, though: the number of taste buds decreases with age. Now you can see why elderly persons season their food more than most. As food tastes less savory, they may eat less, and the possibility of malnourishment increases.

How well can you hear? Humans can monitor the ticking of a watch at 20 feet (assuming it's a quiet room). Hearing is a highly developed sense, even at birth. When most of your bodily functions are at their lowest level of operation, hearing is at its sharpest. At 4 a.m., your hearing sense is responding at its keenest level. This is not far-fetched, in that prehistoric man used this as his radar while he slept. Such a well-developed sense allows mothers to sleep and to monitor newborns. Also, recall that 13 hours later (5 p.m.), your hearing ability peaks again.

Rumor has it that people who are suspicious or slightly paranoid utilize their hearing more efficiently. It could be. Senses mobilized for protection tend to be keener than others.

Any way you look at it, the ability to hear is an excellent example of good vibrations.

The sense of touch allows you to feel the wing of a fly gently falling on your face. The sensitivity of your fingers can detect a vibration of 0.02 micron. In fact, the skin sense has about 200,000 nerve endings for temperature, 500,000 for touch and pressure, and 3,000,000 for pain.

Notice that there are many more pain receptors than for temperature, touch or pressure. There may be a philosophical lesson for that bit of trivia. Selectively, there are 232 pain points per square centimeter behind the knee; 184 per square centimeter on the buttocks; 60 on the thumb pad; and 44 on the tip of the nose. Relatively speaking, pain hurts more behind the knee than on the tip of the nose.

The pain receptors for internal organs are very scattered and are loosely organized. As a result, internal hurt is often transferred to other areas (e.g., angina pain caused by reduced blood flow to the heart is felt in the left shoulder or arm rather than the chest).

There is also a very therapeutic, pleasurable aspect to touching. Gently petting an animal tends to calm your entire body, blood pressure decreases, cardiovascular functioning improves, and your resistance to disease increases. Some researchers have observed that heart rates and brain waves of patients in a deep coma will improve if someone will just hold their hands.

The therapeutic use of touch is not new. It has been depicted in cave paintings dating back 15,000 years. Still, touch is a sense which needs to be used much more frequently. It's just that people are afraid to trust this sense.

With this elementary education of the five basic senses, it's time you discovered the others (since you've been using them your entire life, anyway).

When you are asked to close your eyes and touch your nose with your index finger, you are engaging these special senses. A gymnast rotating through space is relying on these somesthetic senses as much, or more so, than vision. The most routine activities (walking or running) would be impossible without this sense information.

There are sense receptors located in your joints, tendons and muscles which inform your head about various positions and movements of bodily parts. Without this kinesthetic sense, it would be necessary to watch every step you take. You would have to "tell yourself" how to walk. Individuals whose movements have been dramatically impaired as a result of accidents are well aware of the value of this sensory information. For example, when you are asked to "make a muscle," your kinesthetic sense tells you, "It's done." You don't have to look at your arm or touch the muscle to know that you have succeeded.

The vestibular sense signals balance and offers information as your head rotates through space (in relation to gravity). This sensory organ, for the most part, is located in your inner ear. When you are enjoying a ride at an amusement park (particularly a ride that turns you every which way but loose), you are engaging this sense. As you ride in a car or airplane, this sense tells you when you are speeding up or slowing down. This is the mechanism which tells you if you are falling, and it is also the culprit behind motion sickness.

As anyone who has ever had inner-ear trouble can tell you, you can't really appreciate this sense until it acts up and gives you faulty information. We take our balance for granted.

There is talk of another sense: magnetism. Most of this information comes from British zoologists who have studied the animal homing instinct. These researchers have demonstrated that humans, too, may possess an inner compass based on a perception of the earth's magnetic field.

A study was conducted by blindfolding a group of college students and taking them on a 30-mile, winding-road excursion. At the end of their trek, they were asked to point in the direction from which they had come. The results were fascinating. Students were more accurate if they pointed before taking off their blindfolds. As soon as they were allowed to see their surroundings, they became confused. Apparently, too many sensory comments contaminated their judgment.

There are two other magnetic points to be made. The penultimate is that the magnetic sense is somehow "turned off" during sleep. The final point is that either females have a more developed magnetic sense than males, or have learned how to rely better on this sense in order to find their way around.

To summarize, your body takes all the information from all of your senses and puts it together into one neat, clean picture. This information facilitates your wanderings through this existence. Our senses are the road signs. As a result, it is essential that we maintain clear sensory impressions. However, humans contaminate and dull their senses daily by acting as if their bodies were indestructible. Anything you do to your body which interferes with your daily sensory function makes *no sense*. Protecting yourself physically makes good sense — body sense, that is.

References:

Coon, D. *Introduction to Psychology: Exploration and Application*. Los Angeles: West Publishing Company, 1983.

Panati, C. *Breakthroughs*. New York: Berkley Books, 1980.

Rathus, S. *Psychology*. New York: Holt, Rinehart, and Winston, 1981.

Steadman, N. Hands-on healing. *New Body*, 1983, *2*, p. 18ff.

HEARKEN THESE WORDS!

One phrase which strikes fear in the human heart is "Now, I'm only going to say this once..." As a result, the onus of responsibility has been placed upon you to "Get it," "Get it the first time," and "Get it right." Having to "listen" is an uncomfortable responsibility.

Probably one of the most disconcerting feelings results when one walks away from a meeting asking, "What did he say?" Parents constantly complain, "My child doesn't listen." One of the commonest complaints in modern marriage is, "My spouse never talks to me or listens to what I'm saying." Finally, business is also caught in this trap, because the perennial charge is, "The managers (or employees) don't listen to us." In general, the standard complaint if someone doesn't see your side: "He/she doesn't listen."

Hearing is considerably more than a matter of receiving sound waves set up by vibrating bodies in our environment, transmitted through the air to our eardrums, and finally registered by the brain where auditory experiences occur. In fact, here are the statistics.

Humans speak at approximately 120 to 180 words per minute; they think at a rate four or five times that. What psychologists know is that humans spend 80% of their waking hours communicating. Of that time, 45% (or 27 minutes per hour) is spent listening. The bad news is that only 25% (or approximately seven minutes per hour) of the latter amount is devoted to effective listening. Such a deafening deficit costs billions of dollars and countless friends annually because of letters which have to be retyped, time spent redirecting, and personal omissions because one did not hear clearly and accurately.

The bottom line is that listening is a learned behavior. The more it is practiced, the more it is improved. However, our culture teaches us not to question if we do not understand or hear accurately. This is due to the fact that our culture places such a high premium on "authority." In other words, never question someone who knows more than you do. This silent premise was tested.

In one study, 94% of the college students sampled freely admitted that they had failed to understand their professor at least twice in class. Upon further investigation, it was found that 70% acknowledged they would *not* question the professor for clarification. Their reasons: They were afraid of looking conspicuous or stupid. Culture strikes again.

Before you dismiss this study as not applicable, when was the last time you asked your boss to explain the reason for a given set of instructions? When did you last ask a doctor to clarify a diagnosis; a stranger to repeat street directions; or your spouse to elaborate on weekend plans?

It is impossible to tune out friends and "influence" people. Yet, this is a common occurrence. This "tuning-out" or selective attention is referred to as "autistic thinking" (not to be confused with the serious disorder known as autism). Here, selective attention is a perfectly human and normal behavior and refers to "hearing only what one wants to hear."

For instance, bad news may, by necessity, have to be repeated over and over before the recipient will actually hear it. It's almost as if the brain says, "I'll delay your understanding this as long as possible, and then the bad news won't hurt as much."

Another example of autistic thinking is the person who constantly lives in a fantasy world, and refuses to "hear" the outside. To paraphrase, "It's more fun on the inside, and outside's not safe."

In addition to auditing for information and education, hearing is a powerful agent for establishing and maintaining friendship. For instance, listening to another's point of view indirectly informs that they are valued. Based on the psychological principle of "reciprocal reinforcement," listening to and comprehending the other makes people feel good about themselves. People will like you if your behavior makes them feel good.

The following is a list of ways to improve your Listening Retentiveness.

Spend approximately 50% of your conversation time listening to the other person. In addition, be an active (versus passive) listener. Although some will consider this an opportunist attitude, show your interest in the conversation, perhaps adopting a "What's in it for me" stance.

Don't focus on your accomplishments. If you do, you will tend to dominate the conversation, and you diminish the value of the other individual. Moreover, never be judgmental during a conversation. This succeeds in making your friend defensive, and all communication channels (not just listening) break down. Recognize that there are other people in the world in addition to you.

Similar to the above, approval is the best reinforcer. Be careful not to overdo it with praise and compliments. Doing so will imply insincerity.

Take responsibility for the success of the conversation. There are several ways to do this. In addition to being an active participant, make mental notes. After the conversation, write down your responsibilities. In order to train yourself to be a better listener, plan to share the conversation (assuming it is not in confidence) with a colleague within eight hours.

Avoid interrupting. If it is absolutely necessary for you to interrupt another, cushion the distraction with "Pardon me" or "Excuse me." In general, people avoid individuals who have a reputation for interrupting.

Ask questions if you need more information. As discussed previously, asking for clarification may be construed to be a sign of a mature listener. Also, teach your children to ask questions.

Look at the other person. Granted, constant eye-contact tends to make the best of us paranoid; alternate between looking toward the person and direct eye-contact.

Make every attempt to keep the subject and conversation consistent. Listen for central themes, and make your input meaningful.

Identify the purpose of the conversation. Is the goal of the speaker to inform, to persuade, to educate, or to entertain?

Keep your feelings and other distractions in check. If you allow yourself to become too emotionally involved, communication breaks down. Your focus becomes extremely myopic, and you are unable to uphold your conversational contract because your emotions are swaying your judgment.

Finally, don't be afraid to listen to yourself. When you talk over concerns with yourself, you are quite capable of creative problem-solving. So, listen to your own logic and follow the ten rules above. You will find that an interesting side-effect of listening and believing in yourself is that your self-esteem tends to increase dramatically.

To summarize, there are three components to listening: 1. Interpreting the material you hear; 2. Processing, analyzing, synthesizing, and/or retrieving information; which leads to 3. Responding. The difference between a simple and an effective response depends on the accuracy with which you listen.

There is no doubt that listening is one form of caring. It allows you to acknowledge your own self-worth and that of your friend. Effective listening is an escape different from all other "run-away" behaviors. Effective listeners can escape loneliness and enter a circle of friendship.

References:

Montgomery, R.L. "Are You A Good Listener?" *Nation's Business*, 1978, *67*, pp. 52-53.

Lane, M. "Are you 'Really' Listening?" *Reader's Digest*, 1980, *117*, pp. 183-188.

"Secrets of Being a Better Listener, Interview with Lyman K. Steil, an Authority on Communication." *U. S. News and World Report*, 1980, *88*, pp. 65-66.

Williams, R.L., & Long, J.D. *Toward a Self-Managed Life Style.* Boston: Houghton-Mifflin, 1979.

Patterson, C.J. "Teaching Children to Listen." *Today's Education*, 1978, *67*, pp. 52-53.

A CLASS ACT

Class is like intelligence — everybody has some. Moreover, class is like personality — everybody has some of that, too. Finally, class is like your health. No matter how bad your health is, you still have some degree of stamina. So, simply put, everybody's got class (intelligence, personality, and health); it may not be much, but at least you have a place to start.

Then there are those folks (to paraphrase the line from *My Fair Lady)* who "ooze 'class' from every pore." No matter what they say, people listen. No matter what they do, people watch. They are imitated and emulated constantly. If they mess up, they manage to recover with style. They have a charisma about them which causes every head to turn when they enter a room. You long to be with them, because their spotlight is influential to share. They have an elegance, social power, and countenance which is captivating.

Where did they get "it"? Actually, they learned it.

Although many people equate money and class, class cannot be bought. However, there are some parts which can be manufactured. This is not as complicated or as far-fetched as it sounds. For instance, when you plan for an important job interview or function, here's what psychology tells us that humans invariably do.

First, you decide how badly you want the job or how "big of a deal" this meeting is. If you decide that it's important for you to make a "class" statement, then a lot of extra time is absorbed as you select the correct clothing, verbally rehearse yourself in front of a mirror, retype resumes, arrive early, and even decide which book to read in the waiting room (after all, you are what you read). Each behavior is calculated to make a "class" statement about you.

You manufacture or create "the class act" that you want to be — it may or may not be effectively presented. One thing is for sure — that first appearance says more than most people want to believe.

Physical appearance is important for both men and women. However, research (and regrettably, common cultural observation) continues to reveal that physical beauty represents a sexist double standard. To explain, physical beauty for a female is more related to class than for men. Women, if beautiful, are more readily identified as "having class." Men, even if they are not handsome, can obtain class status simply by being successful.

This double standard is changing slightly as women have undoubtedly proven their competence. The fact does stand that attractiveness is positively related to perceptions of class for both men and women.

In addition to physical appearance, there are some things which are not easy to manufacture, but they are equally important in presenting a "class statement." People who are perceived as having class are usually described as intelligent, witty, and honest.

Looking at each of these three, it's difficult (if not impossible) to say which one is the most important or strongest of the class requirements. Each impacts on the other.

Take language, for instance. Even though an outwardly classy appearance can be engineered, opening your mouth is a proof- positive sign of your true "CQ," or Class Quotient.

A personal command of language signals competence and "smarts." Furthermore, we humans attach a great deal of significance not so much on what someone says, but how they say it. Two people can say the exact same thing, but ten times out of ten, only the one who knows how to say it will be heard.

The psychological rule of thumb here is "It really doesn't matter what you say, if you're sure of it, people will listen." So one way to raise your CQ is to increase your vocabulary. Well-read and well-said are fashionable this season.

There is a certain "snobbery of wit" which implies class. Classy humor is well-timed and well-placed; it is sophisticated to the point that you think you "catch on" or grasp the point. Ethnic jokes do not class make. A class wit knows when, where, and how to add humor. The humor is a gentle reminder to everyone present that "class people" are also human.

The rule here is "If no one laughs at your attempted wit, your level of class is suspect."

The ability to relate honestly is essential. If you make an honest statement about yourself, you can never be accused of being something you're not. Although this sounds like a remark from a parent to a child, remember that there is a certain simplicity to class, and honesty is the lowest common denominator. To explain, the honesty which psychologists stress here is not only of thought and word, but in every act and deed. To have class is to present an honest picture of yourself at all times. Think about it — to be a fake is antagonistic to the concept of class.

To gain a further understanding, look at the gains achieved through class. Class grants mobility and allows you to move in and out of all types and levels of circles. You can "hobnob" with the "best" or, if you choose, relate effectively with the "worst." You come across as invulnerable and bigger than life.

Class gives you social power. With it, you can influence directly and indirectly. Assuming you have a reasonable degree of class, you have the power to reward. This type of reinforcer is more important than money. You bestow favors and vicarious success on those with whom you care to associate. People feel good around those people who appear to have a control or "handle" on things.

A person acknowledged as having class is often considered an expert. After all, they've mastered something you may be struggling to obtain.

A person who has class has the ability to influence others. Actually, the weaker person usually wants to do what is asked of him to stay in the other's good graces. It would be very easy to abuse, but remember the true definition of class involves an honest, above-board interaction.

There is a negative associated with class, and at times it is very difficult to understand. A lot of people have a tough time with envy and jealousy, and if you are a respected figure, don't be alarmed when you hear gossip and idle chatter about you. Remember that people without class resort to putting others down in an attempt to raise themselves up. This is a negative side of day-to-day living; don't be alarmed — just know that an honest interaction with others will minimize the problem.

It is possible to raise your "class quotient." Here are some ways.

One does not have to be born with a "silver spoon" in his mouth in order to obtain class. Dollars can't buy class (in spite of what some people believe). It is essential that you believe in your own competence, but remember that you are human and beware of too much ego.

Keep your physical appearance in check. Accentuate your positive features and downplay your "uglies." It is perfectly acceptable to recognize and honestly disguise what you don't want the world to readily see. The *Dress for Success* philosophy works.

Seek out those whom you feel have class. Some of their behavior is bound to rub off on you. Learn as much as you can, because people with similar backgrounds, interests, attitudes, and/or beliefs are attracted to each other.

Develop the ability to relate in an honestly consistent and predictable way. The emphasis here is *honest* which tends to make others see that you are predictable and genuine.

Class can be obtained. And although psychologists don't have an exact definition, class seems to be inextricably related to kindness, consideration, and a general recognition of human worth. This understanding is quite separate and apart from the snob's condescending and/or patronizing attitude.

Finally, true class can be seen in the way you carry yourself. Simply put, feel free to walk as if you love life and all those who surround you. This will put you in a class by yourself.

References:
Mousnier, R. *Social Hierarchies*. New York: Schocken Books, 1973.

Nash, G.B. *Class and Society in Early America*. Englewood Cliffs, N.J.: Prentice-Hall, Inc., 1970.

Sennett, R., & Cobb, J. *The Hidden Injuries of Class*. New York: Alfred A. Knopf, 1972.

Smith, C.M. *Instant Status*. New York: Doubleday & Co., 1972.

MEDITATION: IT'S NO MYSTERY

It doesn't take a guru on a mountaintop to teach you how to meditate. Nor is it necessary to sit cross-legged in a silent and darkened room. Funky clothes, strange charts and other paraphernalia aren't needed, either. Mythology aside, you have all the equipment you need — you have your own built-in meditative device.

Because meditation is as much a feeling as a thought process, it is very difficult to describe. To thoroughly confuse you, meditation may be a nonfeeling/nonthought behavior. Imagine that. And, if at this very moment you are pondering the concept of "nonfeeling/nonthought," then you are indeed meditating.

Everyone has had many varied and fleeting meditative experiences, but most people don't know it at the time. An absorbing hobby which focuses your concentration on a fixed object for a period of time is one example of meditation. As you concentrate, time passes quickly, and you are surprised to realize just how much time has elapsed. Listening to or playing a musical instrument, walking through a park, running, or even watching television are all potential meditative stimuli.

Simply put, meditation is a systematic, organized narrowing of attention. This focused or increased concentration is not only excellent for your mental health, but for your physical health, as well. When you meditate, your body slows down and helps you relax. Therefore, meditation is one technique which alleviates stress.

A standard question is, "What does meditation feel like?" It feels like "nothing" which is actually "something." (Yes, you read that correctly.) This is one time when you want nothing in order to gain health.

To explain, most wince at the idea of mentally achieving or actively thinking about nothing, but sometimes it is essential to "turn down the brightness of the day" and to forget the world.

As one meditator put it: "I meditate to relax, and I relax to meditate. I imagine that I'm walking down a staircase, and with each step that I take I can feel my entire body slowing down. My thoughts slow, and for a brief period — usually about fifteen minutes — I don't have a worry in the world. Many times, after I relax, I can solve problems, finding solutions much more easily. Occasionally I become so relaxed that I think about nothing — absolutely nothing."

There are those avid meditators who strongly affirm that they have more energy, greater concentrative skills and increased alertness. There is some evidence to support these claims, but there are no empirical data to document that meditation increases or expands awareness. That appears to be a strictly personal issue.

There is a great deal of scientific evidence which states that meditation is indeed an effective agent of physiological change. Most of this research was done in the 1970s, and has since been replicated. The findings may surprise you, because meditation's physiological component is striking.

First, regular meditation tends to lower a person's rate of metabolism. This decrease is different from the slowness experienced during sleep. To illustrate, let's look at oxygen consumption. When compared to regular waking hours, you consume ten to 20 percent less oxygen during meditation. This is less consumption than during sleep (eight percent). Respiration and blood pressure also show a substantial decrease. People who meditate at least twice a day tend to have normalized blood pressures throughout their entire lifetimes. Moreover, there is impressive evidence that meditators have a decrease in blood lactate, a substance which has been linked to levels of anxiety. Therefore, meditators may be less anxiety-prone than the average nonmeditating person.

There is also an increase in the brain's alpha waves while meditating. Such a change has been linked to many things — some quite outlandish. However, these waves are generally associated with a much more relaxed body state, daydreaming and drifting thoughts.

So the question remains, "How do you learn to meditate?" There have been many methods used throughout history. Yogis are known to stare intently at various patterns or *mandalas*. The ancient Egyptians stared into oil-burning lamps (hence the origin of the Aladdin fables). Islamic mystics of Turkey achieve a meditative state by whirling 'round and 'round for hours. In the United States, many regularly practice Transcendental Meditation (TM) — a simplified form of meditation brought to this country in 1959 by the Maharishi Mahesh Yogi. All of these approaches encourage a state of relaxation as a result of narrowing of consciousness.

Perhaps the easiest way to learn how to meditate is simply to concentrate on your breathing. But before you start, adopt a passive "take what you get" attitude, and allow whatever will to happen. You will find that the feeling is probably not as dramatic as you would like, but don't limit your expectations to a first experience. Make your environment as quiet and as predictable as possible. Put aside work, telephone calls and appointments. Don't be ashamed to hang a "Meditation in Progress" sign on your door. After you assume a comfortable position, concentrate on your breathing.

Allow your breathing to become relaxed and very natural.

Give your body the freedom it needs to set its own respiration rate, pace and depth. Focus your attention on the act of breathing itself, on the movements of your abdomen, not your nose and throat. If extraneous thoughts enter, refocus your thinking as quickly as possible to the act of breathing, but don't force the issue. If you have an itch, scratch it, but return immediately to your focus of concentration. It's even okay to check your watch (if absolutely necessary). Although this type of intense concentration may be very difficult at first, your brain will soon get the message that you want to narrow your concentration. Once the brain understands what you want, the natural relaxing response follows.

You may want to repeat one word over and over as an aid in helping you relax. People use many words, called *mantras,* with "om," "holy," "easy," "calm," "relax" and "one" as the most frequently used. These words are euphonious, with open vowels and soft consonants; harsh-sounding words are not effective. Although these mantras may sound mysterious, they have no mystical meaning and are only a way to help you concentrate. It doesn't matter which one you choose, or if you choose none of them. (Research informs that they are not necessary.) Merely orienting and reorienting your conscious mind on your breathing will serve the same purpose.

If you want to combine both techniques, then sit quietly in a comfortable position (preferably sitting so you won't fall asleep). Close your eyes and visualize every muscle in your body relaxing. Begin with your feet and slowly move up to your face. Breathe through your nose and become aware of your breathing. As you exhale, say the word "one" (or any other mantra you choose, but repeat the same word throughout the entire meditation) over and over again, silently to yourself. Expect distracting thoughts, and when they "pop in," ignore them and gently reorient your attention on breathing and the word "one."

The first time you meditate, you will probably notice how

incredibly difficult it is to bring your mind into a mode of over-concentration. Your mind will run wild; you will think things you haven't thought of in years. You will hear surrounding sounds, and your mind will be easily distracted. But if you continue this breathing exercise two times a day, five or ten minutes at a time, your mind will eventually concentrate on cue, and then the external world will *not* exist for you. If there is an emergency, you will know it immediately.

To summarize, a relaxed body and brain is certainly a more efficient, productive and creative system. You can meditate anywhere — at your desk, in an airplane, in a hotel room. Most people think that meditation is only valuable when you are upset, but that is just another myth. Meditation is best when implemented consistently, two or three times a day over a long period of time, but you'll see remarkable effects in a much shorter time. Probably one of the best, most effective times to meditate is immediately before an important business meeting. As a result of your meditation, you can look fresh and certainly more relaxed. Furthermore, meditation helps you think clearly.

Meditation is not based on mythological principles. Rather, it is a scientifically proven technique for dealing with stress and coping much more effectively. After all, can you think of a better return on your money? Meditation is free, and it can help alleviate excessive stress which costs big bucks to you and your company.

References:
Benson, H. *The Relaxation Response.* New York: Morrow, 1975.

Campbell, C. Transcendence is as American as Ralph Waldo Emerson. *Psychology Today*, 1974, 7, pp. 37-38.

Carrington, P. *Freedom in Meditation.* New York: Anchor Press/Doubleday, 1977.

Maupin, E.W. Individual differences in response to Zen meditation. *Journal of Consulting Psychology*, 1965, *29*, pp. 139-145.

Wallace, M.A., & Benson, H. The physiology of meditation. *Scientific American*, 1972, *226*, pp. 84-90.

BEDTIME STORIES

Once upon a time, sleep was as simple as a visit from the sandman, and a good night's rest was the norm — not the exception. But if you are one of the 30 million Americans who have a sleep-related problem, then drifting off to never-never land is more of a nightmare than a bedtime story. In fact, half-a- billion dollars a year are spent on drugs to combat "sleep wars" and to help capture that elusive good night's rest.

We spend about one-third of our lives, or roughly twenty-five years, in this strange state of semiconsciousness called sleep. It is not a totally unconscious state, because you can remember your dreams. And this dream state is necessary to maintain the mechanism responsible for long-term memory, stress reduction, and perhaps mental health. Still, no one knows why. After age 16, the quality of sleep begins to deteriorate. Sleep is no longer rejuvenating, but often light and interrupted. It's between middle-to-late adulthood that serious sleep problems surface.

A recent study conducted in the Los Angeles area (representative sample of 1,006 households surveyed) found that 62.1 percent of the individuals had a current or previous sleep disorder. The most frequently cited were nightmares and insomnia.

Two types of nightmares are common. The first, incubus or night terrors (*pavor nocturnus*), is rare. This type of nightmare begins while the individual is in deep, deep sleep and leaves the victim with an intense feeling of horror. The heart rate is markedly retarded, and breathing is quite slow. This problem occurs when the body is at its slowest, apparently triggering one or more brain centers which panic as if the body were being suffocated. Immediately, the body's defenses are mobilized. The pulse rate doubles or triples; breathing is deep and rapid. The hallucination, which usually follows a chilling scream, is that of a wild animal lying on one's chest, sucking life out of its victim: hence the name. The incubus was believed to be an evil spirit which reclined on the sleeper.

Sleepwalking, or sleep-running, is a feature by-product of this type of dream. The person is usually unresponsive to the environment, and experts suggest that the dream must run its course before one is able to awaken. Night terrors are extremely rare in adults; children outgrow the disorder before adolescence. Some researchers suggest that this condition *not* be treated, because most techniques are ineffective and tend to make one more anxious than necessary. Parents usually attach greater significance to the episode than is necessary, exacerbating the problem. Patience, protection, and understanding are essential.

The simple, run-of-the-mill nightmare, unlike the night terror, occurs in the shallowest stage of sleep. It is mild when compared with the stark terror of incubus. It seldom arouses panic, and there are few physiological changes. The dream content is psychological, associated with a chase, free-falling, stabbing, or shooting scenarios. Illness with high fevers and sleeping pills tend to increase the likelihood of these attacks.

Ironically, most people do not realize that the medication they are taking to help them sleep soundly may actually be causing their sleep disturbance. In many cases, the cure is the cause. Sleep medication has a tendency to reduce REM, or rapid-eye-movement sleep — the state at which dreams occur. REM sleep is essential for physical and emotional well-being. As a result, one must "rebound" or compensate for this loss the following night, and then sleep disturbances can occur. The search for a drug which minimizes harmful side-effects continues.

Such an alternative has been studied by somnologists, who are reporting successful use of a food substance, the amino acid called L-tryptophan. Preliminary experimental results suggest that the substance increases length of time spent sleeping, reduces sleep latency (length of time it takes to fall asleep), and does not appear to alter sleep cycles. L-tryptophan is found in milk, eggs, tuna, soybeans, cashews, chicken, turkey, and cottage cheese. If you are dieting, you can also find L- tryptophan in tablet form at your local health food store. This ingredient appears to hold great potential for insomnia sufferers.

Insomnia, the inability to sleep, may be the result of numerous medical, pharmacological, emotional, environmental, or behavioral reasons. The exact cause is unknown. Insomniacs compound their sleep problems through their efforts to somehow force themselves to get to sleep. Rather, all that can be done is to set the stage for sleep by lying down and relaxing when you are tired.

The problem and the cure for insomnia are identical: "Just sleep it off." Currently, the treatment of choice is medication, although as mentioned, some sleeping pills in current use have deleterious side-effects. Although relaxation therapy, behavior modification, and medications have been used to alleviate symptoms, at present there is no one preferred form of treatment. However, individuals who have problems sleeping are encouraged to implement the following: 1. Utilize the bedroom for sleep-related behaviors only, at regular times; 2. Rearrange the bedroom to create a new sleep environment; 3. Adhere consistently to reasonable bedtime and awakening hours; 4. Avoid naps during the day; and 5. Remove distracting stimuli (noise, lights, roommates) around bedtime.

Studies of insomnia have led to investigation of amount of

sleep time needed per evening. It appears that the average sleeper spends seven and a-half hours per evening resting; five percent of the population sleep less than six hours, and another five percent spend more than nine hours daily. Short sleepers average approximately four or five hours per evening. Apparently as they view sleep as being bothersome, they voluntarily cut their sleep time as a result of pressures. Long sleepers sleep approximately nine and a-half hours per evening. These individuals tend to be lengthy sleepers since childhood, seeing sleep as a personal right and privilege. For the sake of trivia, historical evidence suggests that we do not require as much sleep as people living in previous centuries — but then there are many more fun things to do now as compared to the Middle Ages!

Then there is the mirror image of insomnia — narcolepsy. The cause of this disorder is unknown. The symptoms usually begin in adolescence with no antecedent illness. It is a syndrome of recurrent attacks of sleep and is four times more common in men than in women. The condition is characterized by sudden, involuntary attacks of sleep. These episodes usually last about fifteen minutes, after which the person awakes feeling refreshed. The potential hazards and problems result from the unpredictability of the sleep episodes. This problem is currently seen in 100,000 Americans.

An additional, problematic bedtime story is called sleep apnea. This is a condition in which a person stops breathing and gasps for air with loud snores up to several hundred times a night. About 90,000 Americans, mostly overweight and elderly, manifest this disorder. A person suffering from sleep apnea can spend up to 90 percent of sleep time *not* breathing. To say that this problem can affect your cardiovascular system and cause significant physical problems is an understatement. Most individuals who are treated for this problem are under the age of sixty.

Finally, something must be said about snoring. Other sleep

sounds like sighing, murmuring, smacking, and talking, just don't have the potential to irritate (or to fascinate) as a snore. The evidence is not conclusive as to why individuals snore. Statistics inform that 45 percent of normal sleepers snore occasionally, with 25 percent being habitual snorers. Snoring is three times more common in obese individuals. In addition to the social stigma, snoring, which is *not* considered a natural process, may have some definite damaging effects. For instance, complaints of dry mouth and sore throat are common. Other reported problems include fatigue and exhaustion, severe headaches, diseases of teeth and gums, tonsillitis, sinusitis, laryngitis, bronchitis, and serious damage to the hearing mechanism.

Although the cause of snoring is unknown, treatments are common. In fact, more than 300 devices to stop snoring have been registered with the U.S. Patent Office. These include sewing sqeakers into the back of nightwear, tying wrists to the sides of the bed, and, of course, chin straps to keep the mouth shut.

One of the most interesting treatments for snoring was described by Dugas in 1852. He suggested that snoring could be prevented by removing the uvula (the small, fleshy appendage hanging from the middle of the soft palate above the back of the tongue). This procedure was abandoned. It didn't work — patients snored more loudly. Recently, however, a new surgical procedure designed to remove excess palate tissue has been successful 95 percent of the time in either stopping snoring or dramatically decreasing its volume. The best treatment continues to be "Keep your mouth shut." Good advice in all situations.

Although sleep amounts vary, the need for sleep and its potential as a source of comfort or discomfort is present in everyone. It is a basic physiological state and a personal privilege. Sleep restores physiological and psychological functioning; but sleep's by-product, rest, can be contaminated by many problems like medication, anxiety, illness or habit. The key to maximizing sleep potential "rests" upon self-educating and implementing *consistent* sleep habits which satisfy one's own needs.

At present, the cause of most sleep disorders is unknown; however, as one somnologist poetically paraphrased, research appears to have "miles to go before we sleep." Pleasant dreams.

References:
Baekeland, F., & Hartmann, E. The need for sleep. In E. Hartmann (Ed.), *Sleep and Dreaming*. Boston: Little, Brown, 1970.

Bixler, E.O., & et al. Prevalence of sleep disorders in the Los Angeles metropolitan area. *American Journal of Psychiatry*, 1979, *136*, pp. 1257-1262.

Dement, W.C. *Some Must Watch While Some Must Sleep*. San Francisco: W.H. Freeman & Co., 1974.

Out of Your Mind

UNDERSTANDING CREATIVITY

Smile and the world smiles with you; create, and you stand alone. After all, not everyone can write verse like Shakespeare. Unconsciously analyze like Freud. Light up or sound off with bright ideas like Edison. See through things like Madame Curie. Take dance steps like Nijinsky. Provide noteworthy musical works like Beethoven. Or explode on the scene like Nobel. But one thing is for sure: there's a little bit of creativity in everyone.

Take the following test and evaluate your creative quotient. See how much of the creative profile fits you.

1. Do you have a sense of people, events, and problems? In other words, can you read people and understand what makes a person tick?

2. Do you have a large vocabulary? Creators can utilize language as easily as body builders flex their muscles.

3. Do you have a sense of humor? Sometimes creative humor is off-the-wall and hardly funny to the uninitiated.

4. Do you have a high level of energy and "stick-to-itiveness"? Creators tend to be "socialized hyperactives."

5. Are you impatient? Creators tend to have four projects working simultaneously, and are always reading three novels at the same time.

6. Do you have a spontaneous imagination? Exaggerate? Fib? Creative individuals often find the truth boring, and exaggeration much more entertaining and thought provoking.

7. Did you have imaginary companions as a child? For the creative individual, the illusory companion is preferred because he/she is easier to relate to.

8. Are you independent and nonconforming? In other words, do your friends constantly remind you that "You're different!"?

9. Are you uninhibited in your thoughts, feelings and fantasies?

10. Do you enjoy disorder, contradictions and imbalance? Creative people thrive in this type of atmosphere.

For each "yes," score one. The closer your score reaches ten, the better you fit the creative personality stereotype.

In general, people don't really understand creativity; as a result, there are a great many myths surrounding it. For instance, there is a widely held belief that creativity diminishes with age. Not true. Michelangelo began work on St. Peter's Basilica at age 70. Benjamin Franklin was named chief executive of the State of Pennsylvania when he was 79. Goethe wrote *Faust* at the age of 82. Sophocles wrote *Oedipus Rex* when he was 70, and *Electra* at 80. Verdi composed *Othello* when he was 72, *Falstaff* at 77. Laura Ingalls Wilder completed *Little House on the Prairie* when she was 70 (her first book was not published until she was 65). Cecil B. deMille made the movie *The Ten Commandments* when he was 75.

There are many lessons to be learned from Shakespeare's works. Indirectly, he pointed out the relationship between age and creative performance peaks. He wrote his comedies during the first half of his life and the tragedies during the second. Simply put, there are peaks in creative performance in certain age brackets.

Between 20 and 30 years of age, there is a creative performance peak for athletes who participate in physically demanding sports.

Mathematicians may find a creative peak in their 30s, as do practical inventors, most musical composers, movie directors, actors, and athletes in less strenuous sports (e.g., golf).

Writers tend to peak in their 40s. So do architects. Seniority aside, military leadership eventually peaks in the 60-to-70 age bracket. Supreme Court justices and religious leaders tend to emerge in their 70s. (From age 80 on, individuals have the inalienable right to create anything without anyone's permission.)

Another widely held myth concerns the relationship between creativity and intelligence. Intelligence and creativity sometimes — but not always — go hand-in-hand. Persons who are low in intelligence are often low in creativity, but high intelligence is no guarantee of creativity. As a general rule, only moderate intelligence is needed to excel in creative endeavors, especially in fields like art and music. Above a certain IQ(usually 120), intelligence seems to have little relationship with creativity.

Another myth states that creative folks are "crazy." Fractionally true. At times, creative persons give an impression of psychological imbalance, but immature personality traits may just be an extension of a generalized receptiveness to a wider than normal range of experience and behavior patterns. As a general rule, creative persons may have an exceptionally broad and flexible awareness of themselves. They may be more primitive and, at the same time, more cultured; more destructive, and more constructive; madder, yet saner, than the average person. To say that they are less conforming may be an understatement.

So, what is creativity? Frankly, psychologists don't know. It tends to be a type of exceptionally flexible and fluent thinking.

Actually, psychologists are more aware of those factors which *limit* creativity.

First off, emotional barriers tend to make people less creative. These are inhibitions and fears of making oneself look
foolish. The fear of making mistakes, along with excessive self-
criticism, makes one dramatically less productive.

Also, cultural barriers make one less creative. Many
people hold that playfulness is for children only. Not so; creative individuals have an idiosyncratic playfulness all their own.
If you are the sort who believes that only reason, logic and numbers are good, and feelings, intuition, pleasures and humor are
bad , then you may find yourself less creative than your peers.

Then there are the learned barriers. Psychologists refer to
this problem as "functional fixedness." A common manifestation is the attitude that there's only one way to do things — as
a result of social conventions, possibilities, taboos. The way
you know individuals who suffer with this problem is when you
try to introduce something new; they will automatically say,
"We can't do it that way!" Moreover, they will be unable to give
you a reason why. Functional fixedness is tantamount to wear-
ing intellectual and emotional blinders.

Most creative thinkers and other psychologists agree that
there are stages of creative thought. These stages evolved as a
result of interviewing creative individuals and reviewing their
plans of attack to problem-solving. The creators surveyed saw
the first stage as one of orientation. This was the time to define
a problem and to identify its dimensions.

Secondly, overpreparation. At this level, creative thinkers
saturate themselves with as much information relating to the
central problem as possible. This level represents a type of
overkill. But notice that the focus is not on solving the problem
— at least not yet.

At this level, all creative thinkers agree. Following next is
incubation. This is the point when individuals allow the subconscious to work for them. That is, forget the problem for a
while. Let it simmer in the background. Go to a movie. Get

out of the office. Fly a kite. Do anything except worry about the problem.

After the period of incubation, illumination inevitably ensues. It is not unusual for thinkers to report a rapid insight, or series of insights. This "aha" experience is often depicted by an "illuminated" light bulb above a comic-strip character's head.

Next, verification. This is the testing phase to see if the solution really works.

Finally, a crash course in "how to be creative in three easy steps" is presented for your edification. If you want to creatively solve a problem, begin by defining the problem broadly.

If your problem is to design a better doorway, you have indirectly limited the number of solutions. But if you define the problem as, "List all the ways to get through a wall," the number of solutions are creatively infinite. Take the solution and adapt it, modify it, magnify it, minify it, substitute it, rearrange it, and reverse it.

If you want to be creative, make the most out of the atmosphere around you. People tend to be spontaneously original when exposed to others who are creative. If you want to be creative, then spend time with those who are. This is the premise underlying pedagogic standards for art, theatre, dance, and music education. Don't limit creativity to these areas (functional fixedness); business approaches can be creative, too.

As all creative thinkers agree, you must allow time for incubation. Creative thoughts can come out of the blue. All creative thinkers put problems on the "back burner" for a while. They usually allow the answer to come naturally, rather than rushing it.

Look for analogies and relationships between your idea and other problems. Sometimes many new problems are really old problems in disguise. Feel free to historically review and look for precedents.

Remember that no solution is a bad solution; there are only better, more creative solutions. Don't be too hasty to criticize. The presence of criticism or overevaluation is stifling to creative, divergent thinkers. In other words, don't hesitate to go "mental prospecting."

The final section of this article is called the "bottom line" and answers the question: Why aren't more people creative? The answer is best explained by the fact that creativity is drastically reduced by laziness. Clay's Conclusion sums it up best: "Creativity is great; but plagiarism is faster." A lot of people don't want to expend the energy; as a result, some people creatively produce very little.

To conclude, creativity is a combination of intuitiveness, enthusiasm, flexibility, intelligence, independence and initiative. Anyone can have creative ideas, but trusting them and putting them into practice builds creative character. So...go for it!

References:
Crockenburg, S.B. Creativity tests: A boon or boondoggle for children. *Review of Educational Research*, 1972, *42*, pp. 27-45.

Dickson, P. *The Official Explanations*. New York: Delacorte Press, 1980.

Lehman, H.C. *Age and Achievement*. Princeton, N.J.: Princeton University Press, 1953.

Turner, J.S., & Helms, D.A. *Lifespan Development*. New York: Holt, Rinehart and Winston, 1983.

STROKES OF GENIUS

On April 18, 1955, Albert Einstein's 76-year-old brain was donated to science. Researchers hoped to find a physiological substructure responsible for genius. In other words, if there is a biological seat of genius, then surely it would be found in Einstein's brain.

Einstein's brain was indeed different. Researchers found a greater number of cells in critical areas. Within the left parietal lobe, there was a statistically significant ratio of glial cells to neurons. This region is thought to be responsible for the amalgamation of information from other areas of the brain.

Although the discovery of extra glial cells in Einstein's brain was extraordinary, this finding in and of itself is not sufficient to explain genius. In fact, the extra brain development may have been the result of genius rather than the cause of it. At the risk of oversimplifying the issue, genius may be nothing more than a certain style of thinking — a style which is not so very different from that of the common person.

However, due to the mystique and the many myths which have emerged concerning genius, most people believe that they are not capable of advanced thinking. In other words, there are many would-be geniuses who fall victim to the numerous myths and fail to live up to their ultimate potential.

If you were to survey beliefs and attitudes concerning genius, the following opinions would be pervasive. None are true, but because they are perceived as correct, they have a powerful hold and a negative impact on our ability to work, play, and grow both intellectually and emotionally.

Myth: A genius creates masterpieces with a single brush stroke, or invents revolutionary theorems overnight. Not true. Much like any average person, a genius develops ideas via incremental, critical thinking and a special type of worry.

For example, there is no doubt that Ludwig von Beethoven was a genius. But when his music is performed, we do not think of the inordinate amount of work that went into the piece. After all, the believable myth suggests that his creation of a symphony was not difficult at all. Yet, upon inspection of his sketchbooks, over 5,000 pages of preliminary musical themes, phrases, and revisions make it clear that Beethoven worked hard to perfect his genius.

Inherent in this myth is the fact that creative solutions can come "out of the blue," or in an all-of-a-sudden, "aha" experience. The latest research is suggesting that this is not the case at all.

It appears that efficient problem-solvers "creatively worry" and carry a problem around with them even while doing other tasks. Brief episodes of mulling over a problem or creatively worrying about it is a precursor to insight, or the "aha" experience. What appears to be a sudden solution is actually the result of days or weeks of creative worry, detailed thoughts, incremental changes, and critical evaluations — all adding up and eventually allowing the solution to "pop" in.

There is a new twist to this idea of creative worrying. Researchers have found that the genius style of thinking is very critical. As a result, it goes beyond what is commonly referred to as "brainstorming."

In the early 1950s, Alex Osborn developed the notion of brainstorming, initially designed to increase the creativity of American scientists and engineers. The technique allows any idea to be put on the table. Criticism is not allowed; bizarre ideas are welcome; quantity is encouraged; and no critiquing takes place until the ideas are generated. Recent studies have compared brainstorming groups and critical-thinking groups. The result supports the genius way of thinking.

Two groups of undergraduate students were chosen as participants. Both groups were asked to invent brand names for a deodorant and an automobile. One group was allowed to use the brainstorming technique with no instructions. The other group, critical-thinkers, were offered instructions which placed more emphasis on analyzing the ideas as they were produced. The names generated were then rated on a quality scale by another group of students.

As was expected, the brainstorming groups generated more ideas than the critical groups. However, upon closer inspection, they did not create as many "good" ideas. Although the critical-thinking group had fewer ideas, they had the same number of quality ideas. In other words, critical evaluation, or creative worrying, increases the average quality of ideas. Critical judgment is essential from the moment the idea is conceived, and is what separates good ideas from genius-type ones.

Wolfgang Amadeus Mozart's genius is an excellent example of incremental revisions, creative worrying, and critical analysis. Although the recent stage play and movie depicted Mozart's ability to write masterpieces with ease, there is evidence that this may not be the case. Mozart's notebooks are full of compositions that were begun and not completed, suggesting that he didn't write as easily as many believe. However, Mozart had an excellent memory. He was able to critically evaluate, revise, and creatively worry all in his head. In other words, the musical works had been worked and reworked mentally, long before a note hit the paper.

Myth: Geniuses are born. Fractionally true. Although heredity may provide intellectual prewiring, there is evidence to suggest that a genius' abilities are due to practice. In fact, ten years of practice seems to be the amount required.

Although Mozart began his musical career at the age of four and wrote his first symphony at the age of eight, he is not remembered for his earlier works. Approximately 12 percent of Mozart's musical compositions were composed within the first ten years of his career; however, only five percent of them are acknowledged in artistic renditions and recordings today.

Musicologists agree that Mozart's early works are of a lower quality than were his later works. To test this idea further, 75 well-known composers were evaluated. From this group, only five percent produced acknowledged masterpieces within the first ten years of their musical careers. Their finest creations came after ten years in the profession.

A period of time is needed to learn the rules of the trade. Even a would-be genius must study and learn the necessary building blocks. For instance, it is estimated that a master chess player must develop at least 50,000 patterns, with four or five pieces in each pattern. These building blocks have been developed over time: ten years and 25,000 to 30,000 hours of creative worrying and actively studying chess.

Also relating to amount of practice is the would-be genius' motivational level. In Western culture, particularly, influential artists and scientists are known for their long careers, extraordinary productivity, and total commitment to their work. For example, in a 45-year career, Sigmund Freud produced 330 publications. Over a 75-year artistic career, Pablo Picasso painted several thousand works. Albert Einstein wrote 248 pieces over a 53-year period. Motivation and commitment are key variables in the definition of genius.

Myth: An individual genius is consistently creative throughout his or her life. Not so. Leonardo da Vinci, acknowledged genius who lived a life of extraordinary creativity, spent years trying to develop a flying machine which flapped its wings. Additionally, he developed a new method of painting on plaster which allowed him to paint at a more leisurely pace. Unfortunately, the paint faded prematurely. The result is that his painting, *The Last Supper*, is in very poor condition today.

It is hard to believe, but Einstein rejected the statistical laws of quantum mechanics — the laws which are currently accepted by physicists in their conception of the universe. Even though quantum physics came about as an extension of Einstein's work, his rejection of it removed him from the forefront. In later life, Einstein himself stated that this inability to see far enough into the future made him and his views a "genuine old museum piece."

The point here is that a genius, just like a person with average intelligence, often makes mistakes.

Myth: An intellectual genius does not waste time. Not so. Sir Isaac Newton, who invented calculus and developed seminal works in physics, spent 25 years studying alchemy. He wrote thousands of pages in search of mysterious elixirs and forces which influence nature. Franz Joseph Gall, a pioneer in the study of the brain, is also known for his development of phrenology — the pseudoscientific theory that mental development and personality can be determined by the bumps on one's head. Another example of genius gone astray is Alfred Russel Wallace, who, independently of Charles Darwin, developed a theory of natural selection. He also spent many years "communicating" with the dead.

Myth: To be a genius, one must create original works. Not true. Take Johann Sebastian Bach, for instance. At the height of his career, he was commissioned to produce one cantata for each week of the year and an additional one for holidays. In a typical year, he wrote 60 pieces. In five years, he composed approximately 300 cantatas. To meet the demand, Bach borrowed from his own earlier works, folk songs, and other published pieces. One researcher has found that many of Bach's works were borrowed from other composers, notably Antonio Vivaldi.

Bach was not unique in his borrowing. George Frideric Handel, another master of the baroque era, used and embellished themes written by Georg Philipp Telemann. Mozart was also impressed by other musicians' works. One musicologist estimates that several of Mozart's melodies appeared in the compositions of his peers, suggesting that embellishing others' works was common.

This is not the same as plagiarizing. In each of the above cases, the genius lay in the ability to take or to borrow from another and make it much finer.

Myth: Genius is always respected and acknowledged. Not so. The title, "genius," is often bestowed after the person's lifetime. Once again, Bach is an excellent example. In 1750, when Bach died, his works passed in popularity with him. His music was ignored for almost 75 years. He was considered old-fashioned and referred to as "the old wig." It was not until this century that musicians returned to Bach, acknowledged his genius, and performed his works in the manner he prescribed.

The point here is critical: What is genius in one set of circumstances may be simple mediocrity in another. In other words, the acknowledgment of genius is an interaction between the artistic work or scientific theory and the current needs of the audience.

Although no one knows for sure, perhaps Einstein's extra glial cells were the result of years of dedicated creative worry, detailed analysis, and revisionary thinking. Add to that practice, continuous study, and a high level of commitment, and you have the individual component necessary for genius.

Finally, it could be that you are smart enough to take into account the sensitivity of the public and create the product, scientific theorem, or artistic masterpiece which fits the audience's needs, then you may deserve the title, "genius."

References:
Building a better brain. *Longevity,* November, 1986, *1*, pp. 1-3.

DeGrott, A. (1966) Perception and memory versus thought: Some old ideas and recent findings. In B. Kleinmuntz (ed.) *Problem Solving: Research, Method, and Theory.* New York: John Wiley, pp. 19-50.

John-Steiner, V. *Notebooks of the Mind.* Albuquerque: University of New Mexico Press, 1985.

Weisberg, R.W. *Genius and Other Myths.* New York: W.H. Freeman and Company, 1986.

Weisskopf-Joelson, E., & Eliseo, T.S. An experimental study of the effectiveness of brainstorming. *Journal of Applied Psychology,* 1961, *45*, pp. 45-49.

Yulsman, T. Einstein update: The better brain. *Science Digest*, July, 1985, *93*, p. 53.

ATTENTION, PLEASE

What do a typical soldier standing guard, a lifeguard working at the beach, a doctor monitoring vital life signs, and a student listening to a lecture have in common? At most, between 20 and 30 minutes of effective concentration before their attentive skills vanish. In fact, for most people, half of their attention span is lost within the first 15 minutes. And, to take it a step further, if the task requiring close scrutiny is extremely difficult, the ability to concentrate can be lost within the first five minutes.

Because humans are constantly barraged by sensory input — sights, smells, and skin sensations — the odds are against sustaining an effective level of concentration. The brain is constantly screening information, deciding what is useful and important. As a result, the process of concentrating takes second priority. In fact, the human brain is just not wired to concentrate for long periods of time — at least not without a little help.

Psychobiologists have recently discovered that the ability to concentrate, pay attention, or remain "vigilant" occurs at many brain levels. What was once thought to be a purely conscious function may actually start in the more primitive, unconscious, life-sustaining part of the brain.

Researchers have known for years that humans see what they want to see and hear what they choose to hear. However, this process of selective attention has never been clearly understood. In fact, the exact physiological process continues to evade scientists. As a result, the ability to concentrate, to focus, and to screen out extraneous sensory input was thought to be a function of the brain's more complex processing centers. Evidence now suggests that the screening actually begins before the signals reach the "thinking" part of the brain.

To demonstrate, researchers measured the electrical activity of nerve cells that receive input from the face's pain receptors. These cells, located in the lower brain area (dorsal horn of the medulla) are similar to those spinal cord cells which respond to pain in other parts of the body. In this preliminary study, monkeys were taught to pay attention to one of two stimuli: either a light, or heat blown on the face. When the monkeys were rewarded for responding to heat, the electrical activity in these lower brain cells increased. When the monkeys were taught to respond to the light cue, even though the heat on their faces was present, the lower brain cells responded with half the intensity.

Although the research seems complicated, the finding is simple: the ability to concentrate effectively involves many levels of brain function.

Although pseudoconcentration at the lower brain level is a new finding, researchers have known for years that the brain is equipped with an arousal center which controls alertness. Common sense would suggest that an arousal mechanism would also work to achieve an effective level of concentration. Unfortunately, this bundle of nerve fibers, the reticular activating system, prefers change and works best when stimulated from various sources. It does not work well with routine regimented behaviors. As a result, the arousal center does not facilitate concentration.

To concentrate, some tasks must be repeated over and over

until a person "gets" it. This repetitiveness is interpreted by the brain as a decrease in activity; the result is a simultaneous decrease in the arousal system in the brain and body. Moreover, other low arousal signs emerge, including drowsiness and decreases in efficiency, adrenaline, and electrical patterns in the brain which simulate sleepiness. At its extreme, three out of 100 individuals develop a condition called "Attention Deficit Disorder" (ADD).

The psychological factors underlying a person's ability to concentrate have been a source of study for years. A great deal of research has been generated to ascertain why people fail regularly when given routine, repetitive tasks. In other words, if simple regimented behaviors are so easy, why do people make so many mistakes in the process? What makes them lose their focus or concentration?

The modern study of concentration began in Great Britain in World War II. At that time, the Royal Air Force wanted to know why radar operators failed to detect obvious "blips" on their screens. As a result, enemy vessels went undetected, rendering British ships vulnerable.

To solve the problem, air force cadets participated in a study whose results have been duplicated repeatedly. The participants were asked to observe a pointer move about the circumference of a clock. However, the clock had no hour or minute markings. Normally, the pointer jumped the equivalent of one second; the task was to identify when the pointer moved twice as far. Performance was initially quite high, but deteriorated precipitously in speed and accuracy as the task continued.

Since this initial project, hundreds of studies have confirmed this concentration drop within the first 30 minutes. It is an accepted finding that 20 to 30 minutes is the optimal time that a person is able to concentrate, without making errors, on visual or auditory stimuli. This finding is constant for students listening to a lecture, an inspector monitoring a computer screen, or a surgeon following a complicated procedure.

Fortunately, with each new study, researchers have identified additional psychological components which influence one's ability to concentrate and increase this 30-minute limit. These factors include: hunger, noise, anxiety, time of day, pace, complexity/change, and feedback.

Many people are aware that their ability to concentrate slips after eating. Particularly during the workday, managers are well aware of "post-lunch dips" in both productivity and concentration among employees.

One research study tested 23 undergraduate students and their ability to concentrate and to accomplish a repetitive task. Each participant attended one eight-hour day session subsequently followed by a similar night session. At the middle of both day and night sessions, a full meal was served. To add a psychological twist, half of the subjects were tested under noisy conditions, and the remainder in a quiet environment. The researchers also looked at their anxiety levels.

There was a post-meal dip in concentration both for the day and evening sessions. On a task which required them to identify sequences of numbers, all students were correct 65 percent of the time; however, there was a nine percent drop in effectiveness after eating. When the students' accuracy was assessed based on a noisy or quiet environment, the results were surprising.

Those who completed the task in a noisy environment, after eating, suffered only a three percent dip in accuracy. For those in a quiet environment, there was a 16 percent drop. Apparently, the subjects had to overcompensate and coach themselves to be vigilant at the task in order to overcome the noise. This study suggests that eating decreases concentration, and the presence of noise causes minimal stress which, when overcome, improves concentration.

When it comes to concentration, anxiety is a two-edged sword. Some studies, like this one, have shown that mild stress or anxiety improves vigilance. Another study found that working in a slightly warm environment provoked discomfort, which increased anxiety, and improved production.

Concentration itself has been found to cause anxiety. In fact, one study found that the pressure resulting from concentration and vigilance is a common denominator and equally stressful for Type A (rushed, competitive) and Type B (laid-back, relaxed) individuals. Assuming this is true, this discomfort may explain why people avoid tasks which require concentration and look for quick solutions rather than adequately dealing with a problem or searching for a new procedure.

Concentration has also been linked to time of day, specifically, the body's circadians or daily cycles. Many physiological processes (body temperature, hormone production, pain perception) operate on a 24-hour up-and-down cycle. For instance, body temperature is at its lowest point between 4 a.m. and 7 a.m. and at its highest point about 12 hours later. One's concentration level also fits a rhythmic cycle.

Psychologists have categorized most concentration tasks as either "successive" or "simultaneous." In a successive task, a person compares something to previously memorized information. An inspector who compares a product to an established standard uses successive concentration skills.

Simultaneous concentration does not require memory. All the information needed to answer the question is right before you. An example would be an automobile inspector who looks for cracks or damage in the product.

With these two types of tasks in mind, researchers have shown that the ability to effectively complete successive concentration tasks — those involving comparison and memory — peaks in the morning; whereas concentration during simultaneous tasks — those where all the facts are directly before you — peaks in the afternoon.

Pace, complexity, and change have also been identified as variables which affect one's ability to concentrate.

An optimum pace while performing a task facilitates concentration. Too fast leads to error. Too slow leads to boredom. The same is true with complexity. If the task is too easy or difficult, focus and concentration break down.

Making tasks sufficiently complex and challenging improves vigilance. To take it a step further, if a person is required to concentrate on too many factors at one time, all concentration breaks down.

Concerning change, the arousal center likes varied input and stimuli. One study required participants to monitor sounds. Within 30 minutes, concentration skills vanished. However, when the researchers varied the sounds unpredictably from one ear to the other, the subject was able to monitor vigilantly for longer than 30 minutes.

Finally, specific feedback is linked with a person's ability to concentrate effectively. This is not a complicated concept. When a person knows how he or she is doing with a task, he or she is better able to complete the project successfully.

To elaborate, one researcher asked people to monitor length of vertical lines. Based on their performance, they were given three kinds of feedback. First, when they correctly identified a line, they heard a tone. Second, if they identified a line as a correct one which did not fit the established length, the tone sounded. Third, if they missed a vertical line totally, they heard a tone. The researcher found that the first and second tone as feedback kept concentration and vigilance high. Knowing that they had missed one completely did not raise or lower vigilance skills.

The following are several behavioral tricks which can help concentration:

Maintain a mild stress or anxiety level. A perceived need or personal pressure can help maintain your acuity and concentration in order to get the job finished. If you are comfortable with deadlines, impose one and get the job finished.

Take breaks every 20 or 30 minutes. The level of attention decreases after approximately 30 minutes of intense work — and the brain's arousal center prefers change.

Work at a realistic pace and don't get in over your head. An optimum rate of work facilitates concentration. Break the project down into little projects and complete one at a time.

Avoid big meals during the day. If a project is due which requires intense concentration and vigilance, you may not have the advantage of enjoying a big lunch. Post-meal slumps are real and eat into your concentration time. To maximize your working time and minimize post-lunch syndrome, eat several small meals during the day.

Put sound in your work environment. It seems to be a myth that people concentrate best in quiet environments. Noise and other sounds facilitate vigilance. To improve your concentration, add music to the background, or leave the door open so that you can hear what's going on.

Prompt yourself. Feedback facilitates concentration. Tell yourself when you have done a good job or materialized a correct solution. But most important of all: when you catch your mind wandering, gently guide your mental powers back to the task at hand.

References:
Carpenter, E. New measures of attention. *Psychology Today*, 1985, *19*, p. 20.

Lowe, G. Food for thought. *Psychology Today*, 1987, *21*, p. 14.

Miller, J.A. Paying attention at many levels. *Science News*, November 9, 1985, *128*, pp. 295-296.

Warm, J.S., & Dember, W.N. Awake at the switch. *Psychology Today*, 1986, *20*, pp. 46-53.

IMAGINE THAT!

Most people are not aware of how powerful imagination can be in daily living. It is a magnificent coping mechanism and problem- solving tool, and aids in creativity. In fact, there is no man- made device or invention which can rival the power, flexibility, ease, and magic of the mental image. It simply needs to be used.

The most astounding research finding concerning imagination is the fact that the brain perceives the real world and the imagined world in exactly the same way. Not only has this been demonstrated experimentally, but it has also been shown that brain-damaged individuals who lose some of their perceptive abilities also lose corresponding imagination skills. Additionally, illusions dealt with through the senses will also be seen as illusions when they are imagined.

To explain, studies completed in 1910 and repeated in 1970 hypothesized that if imagery and perceptions are similar, then one would interfere with the other. In one experiment, subjects were asked to form a mental picture of a flower or to create an auditory mental image similar to the sound of a telephone. While participants were actively imagining, either a faint geometric figure was projected to them or a sound presented in the outside world. In these situations, subjects were not as responsive to outside stimuli that was projected or heard. Mental images interfered with perception, and auditory images interfered with hearing. Although this is a commonsense finding, it does demonstrate the similarity between imaging and perception, as well as the power of mental images.

To take it a step further, if mental imagery and perception are similar to each other, are they both altered in patients who have suffered brain damage? The answer is yes.

In cases where the brain has been disturbed (e.g. stroke or brain injury), and brain cells in a specific region of the right hemisphere have been destroyed, some patients will develop a condition called "visual neglect." As a result, they may "ignore" everything on the left side.

If a patient with this condition were asked to imagine standing at the end of a room which he knows well and to describe everything he sees, he will mention only the things on the right. If you tell this same patient to imagine walking to the other side of the room, turn around, and describe what he sees, he will continue to see only things on the right. However, because he has turned around, he will see those objects previously ignored because they were originally on his left side. Damage to the brain's perceptive ability affects the brain's imaginative powers, as well.

If the brain sees imagery and perceptions in a similar way, does this also hold true for imagined, as well as perceived illusions? Once again, the answer is yes.

There is a well-known illusion which has to do with contrasting weights. A person initially lifts a very heavy object in one hand and a very light one in the other. The participant is then asked which one is heavier. Of course, the answer is obvious. Next, the subject is given two new weights, both weighing the same. The participant is then asked to identify the heavier of the two. If the left hand held the heavy object originally, the object (although of equal weight) now held in this hand will be perceived as lighter than the object in the right hand.

Now, a twist . One experimenter asked a participant to

imagine holding two balls of different weights. After the person created the mental image and held it internally for a short period of time, he was handed two real balls of equal weight. Then he was asked which of the two was heavier. The subject reported the same illusion even though he had imagined the first set of weights.

Since imagination and perceptions are similar, is it possible to substitute imaginative action for real practice? Once again, the answer is yes.

To test this idea, a group of students was recruited to participate in an experiment. They were asked to mentally rehearse a simple gymnastics exercise. Five minutes a day for six consecutive days, the participants, who had no gymnastics experience, imagined themselves exercising on a horizontal bar.

Following the six days of mental rehearsal, the subjects were asked to physically perform the mental exercise. The experimental findings supported the fact that imagery was an effective means of practicing. Participants with more vivid, controlled imagery performed better than those with less-acute imaging abilities. The experimenters extrapolated the finding further. They concluded that mental practice is better than no practice, but actual physical practice is best.

Given the similarity of imagination and perception along with the power of a mental image to stand-in for the real thing, it follows that guided imagery or imagination can be an effective tool in facilitating learning. There is experimental evidence to support this point of view.

To demonstrate the role of imagination in learning, 268 students were recruited. They were led to believe that the study would evaluate the role of television as a learning device. Half of the students watched a video of a lecture which used simple but attractive props and illustrations. The other half, the experimental group, received the same lecture material coupled with a multisensory, imaginary experience. In other words, instead of simply studying and viewing brain-anatomy diagrams, the students were encouraged to imagine themselves as neurons "floating" around inside the brain.

At the end of the video sessions, both groups were tested to measure immediate recall. Another test occurred eight weeks later. Once again, those who used mental imagery had 26 percent better long-term retention than the students who viewed the more conventional approach. The point is clear. Imagination allows one to invent a vivid, memorable experience which creates a type of "ownership" of the material.

Almost everyone has the ability to use imagination. In fact, nine out of ten individuals have no trouble imagining scenes or images on their mental blackboards. For these people, a vivid imagination is a precursor for creative ideas, artistic inspirations, and solutions to problems. If, however, a person tends to use imagination negatively, the results can be just as real.

Remember that the brain treats mental images and perceptions similarly. Remember, too, that mental images can interfere with accurate perceptions. Moreover, a negative imagination can stand-in or substitute for the real thing when the stimulus is not present; therefore, it is possible to create more emotional (and even physical) pain than is objectively necessary. As a result, it is essential to learn how to control your imagination instead of it controlling you.

To reduce a negative imagination to manageable size, remember that you are in charge of your imagination. Even if the images are spontaneous and appear to have a mind of their own, they can be directed. To keep your imagination in check, simply ask yourself the following question: "Is what I'm imagining true?" If it is, you are on the right track. If, however, your imagination is lying to you, making things appear more negative than they really are, blowing the problem out of proportion, and/or creating uncomfortable emotions, then rewrite the mental images to reflect positive solutions and outcomes.

Additionally, imagination can be used as a means of reducing stress. For example, while sitting at your office, take a mental "break" and go to the beach, visit with a loved one, or play golf. Work with your imagination to make the images as vivid as possible. Daydreams and imagination breaks used in moderation are very healthy and effective escapes.

To use imagination as a way to solve problems and facilitate creativity, remember that images occur in a mental medium which acts like a screen. As a result, the image can be manipulated much easier than the physical objects it represents. So, use your imagination to zoom in or shrink an object or problem to manageable size. You may even want to add color. Problems look different when imaginative lights and colors are added. Remove drab and dreary mental shadows by adding light and colors like blue, yellow, and green. The more shape, movement, and color you add, the greater number of solutions you can generate. By imagining as many creative alternatives as possible, you improve your chances of selecting the right problem-solving approach.

As a general rule, imagination and creativity are inextricably linked. However, there are three occasions when there is no relationship between the two: while experiencing a high fever, taking prescribed and nonprescribed drugs, and during childhood. But, for the most part, imagination and creativity are best friends.

To improve your creative skills, simply imagine possibilities. To do that, creative folks are constantly asking themselves "What if?" and then imagining the answers or outcomes to the question. This stimulates a verbal dialogue with yourself, allowing your imagination to fill in the pictures. Let your imagination run free — don't censor it. One other point: always try to imagine one solution or idea beyond what you think will solve the problem. By doing this, you will guard yourself from giving up prematurely. If, however, you are out of practice and you think that your imagination has taken an early retirement, don't panic. Gently prod your imagination to restore its power.

The psychology of imagination is a relatively new area of study. In fact, researchers have learned more about imagery during the past 15 years than in the last several centuries. One point has emerged: imagination is a powerful tool, and, when used effectively, can provide free vacations from a mundane office, reduce stress, and offer inexpensive solutions to potentially expensive problems.

References:

Kosslyn, S.M. Stalking the mental image. *Psychology Today*, 1985, *19*, pp. 23-28.

Shepard, R., Downing, C., & Putnam, T. Inner visions. *Psychology Today*, 1985, *19*, pp. 66-69.

Trotter, R. J. Better learning - imagine that. *Psychology Today*, 1985, *19*, p.22.

EXPERTS: WHO SAYS?

It's time to take a good look at what an expert *really* is.

Our culture places a great deal of trust in experts. As a result, educators believe that this emphasis is due to practice drills and other rote learning techniques common in educational settings. In other words, the expert is different from the average person in his or her ability to apply knowledge rather than just throw out information. Additionally, the current focus on the need for minimum or basic standards while competition continues to increase creates a fascination for those who master specific sets of knowledge.

As the culture becomes more complex, technological change even more common, and information more technical, the value of the expert will increase. Whatever the reason, the need for the expert and the belief in his or her ability is a defined and integral part of our culture.

Experts are special-purpose creatures. By definition, they must know all that there is to know in a specific field. They have an idiosyncratic set of methods, technologies, information sources, and support not available to the uninitiated. The area of expertise is strictly defined, and there is a "rite of passage" which must be satisfactorily completed before the title "expert" is bestowed.

Psychologists have identified the stages of mastery. These levels are: 1. beginner, 2. apprentice, 3. journeyman, 4. artisan, and 5. expert. Although some of these terms are archaic, there is a learned, methodical approach by which one solves a problem or accomplishes an expert task. Ultimately, it is this psychological approach which separates the beginner from the expert. But first, the individual must develop an adequate knowledge base before other expert tricks and approaches are used.

Whether novice or rookie, the would-be expert must start at the beginning. At this stage, the individual begins to study objective facts. The beginner can only apply a specific rule to a given situation. For example, a person learning to drive a stick-shift automobile must be told at what RPM gears are changed. The chess player is more aware of the rules concerning piece movement, and higher strategies are meaningless. In other words, the beginner is so caught up in following, understanding, and mastering rules that he or she cannot see the bigger picture. Rules are necessary; but time, which allows the accumulation of experience, is essential.

With time, experience, and knowledge, the person moves to stage two: apprentice. Performance improves, and the individual learns how to deal with "would be" situations rather than concrete ones exclusively. Gears are changed based on sound, and game players are aware of those situations in which their actions may cause them to lose points.

In this area, the value of the teacher or role model is crucial. The story is told of Charles Darwin, who was a lackadaisical child intellectually until he met a teacher who, like a master craftsman to an apprentice, was able to stimulate his abilities. It was Cambridge tutor, J.S. Henslow, who directed, stimulated, and pushed young Darwin, focusing his interest on the biological sciences. The value of experience and guidance by a revered teacher is crucial.

The third stage, journeyman, is the individual's first attempt to stand alone with some degree of competence. Within this stage, experience accumulates so that journeymen are able to take a task apart, piece by piece. Additionally, they are able to organize the situation in such a way as to categorize the parts in order of importance. Within this stage, they begin to lose some objectivity and can see things subjectively — and, to some degree, intuitively. They will take a calculated risk, because they are aware of past experience as a vehicle to solve current problems.

The fourth stage, artisan, is very close to the actual expert level itself. Within this level, the art of expert problem-solving begins to emerge. The skill becomes rapid, fluid, and intuitive. Immediately, the core of the task stands out, and incidental points are relegated to the background. Again, experience is the key. There are enough "similar" past situations to trigger successful plans.

When the individual reaches the fifth level, he or she is considered an expert. After years of experience and movement through the other four levels, experts do not consciously apply rules, reduce things into parts, or even consciously solve problems. They automatically respond to similarities which trigger correct solutions. The skill is second nature.

Although several of these stages are similar, the critical ingredient is time. The accumulation of experience (usually is about ten years) is crucial to the mastery of any task. But a strong knowledge base is not enough. If you would like to become an expert's expert, it takes more.

In addition to a substantive base of information, there are three skills which are essential to manipulate knowledge. These are the ability to: 1. perceive large blocks of information at a single glance, 2. visualize the problem and alternative solutions before implementation, and 3. understand the concept of "right place, right time, right move."

It doesn't matter if the individual is an expert business executive, lawyer, teacher, nurse, surgeon, cab driver, or athlete. Each one, regardless of complexity, is able to take in, categorize, and organize large blocks of information quickly and accurately.

In a recent study which investigated expert cab drivers, researchers found that their knowledge base was organized hierarchically, like an inverted wedding cake. They first see the big picture, then slowly reduce the facts from large geographic areas to specific areas of town.

One technique in perceiving large blocks of information is to categorize and organize according to priorities. In a recent study, participants were asked to categorize and sort approximately 20 physics problems. Their task was to identify as quickly as possible how they should be solved. Subjects (depending on years of study) were divided into beginners and experts. There were striking differences in the way the two groups perceived the problem.

The beginners sorted according to superficial or basic rules. The more advanced participants were able to see beyond the more basic principles and problem-solve according to deeper, intuitive categories. The experts' sorting abilities allowed them to move from the top of the inverted wedding cake to the bottom with greater ease and less effort. They found a common thread, category, theme, theory, or philosophy which operated like a mental superhighway, allowing the expert to move through complex material with greater speed and less difficulty.

Other studies have been done using athletes and chess players as subjects. Although considered cultural opposites, experts in both fields used identical problem-solving skills. They were able to take large units of behavior, sort them, categorize them, and combine the information into meaningful units.

How is any expert able to categorize and organize so rapidly? Obviously, practice over time accounts for a large part of the ability, but there is more - the ability to visualize or mentally represent the problem.

A recent study was conducted with expert Japanese abacus operators. An abacus is a counting board or frame with beads or balls that slide back and forth on wires or in slots. It is used to teach basic arithmetic, but there are those who can use the abacus with greater alacrity than with modern calculators.

In this study, teenagers, rated as expert abacus operators, were tested. They were given varying restrictions and also distractions. Individuals who were slightly below the expert level seemed to have the most trouble when distractions were created. When the abacus was removed, and the subject forced to solve the problem mentally, "almost" experts moved their fingers as if they were manipulating a real abacus. This was not seen in true abacus experts. In fact, 90 percent of the expert group could calculate as rapidly without an abacus. They did not rely on their fingers or other external crutches. They visualized an abacus which served the purpose just like a tangible one.

One researcher studying chess players found similar proof of the expert use of mental representations. The experimenter noticed that expert chess players had unusual eye movements. Upon further investigation, it was apparent that the chess players' eye movements were a physical manifestation of the individual's mental manipulation of the pieces. They were mentally searching through their store of knowledge in an attempt to discover checkmate combinations. The visualization or mental representation was a technique that the master chess player used to summon old thoughts and situations in order to resolve the current dilemma. The mental representations served as devices for summoning and/or recognizing meaningful board positions (estimated to be at least 100,000 moves) previously stored in the memory.

The expert must understand the concept of "right place, right time, right move." There is an interactive relationship, and psychologists refer to this as the roll of "co-incidence."

The concept of co-incidence has several components. First, the right place. Over the past 20 years, more than 50 percent of the top chess players have come from New York, Los Angeles, and San Francisco. In addition to a strong knowledge base, as well as the ability to perceive and visualize, the expert must consciously select the place which will offer the most support and visibility. A computer expert or business executive is not a necessary commodity in rural areas.

Next, the right time. Experts abounded during the Renaissance period as never before or since. At the turn of this century, Vienna flourished with Sigmund Freud, Ludwig Wittgenstein, Ernst Mach, Arnold Schonberg, and Arthur Schopenhauer. Currently, Silicon Valley in California and Route 128 in Massachusetts are the centers for much of our microchip technology and have been over the past 20 years. As a result, there is a technological and cultural, as well as cultural dictate operating. Experts come and go, depending on the demands at any one point in the technological lifeline.

Finally, the expert who understands risk is aware that making the "right move" is never a known feature of the present. However, the expert is able to minimize risk. Decisions are based on the needs of the present and future. As a result, the true expert is able to pull knowledge from the past, plan for the present, and develop for the future.

References:
Chance, P. Mastery of mastery. *Psychology Today*, 1987, *21*, pp. 43-46.

Feldman, D., & Goldsmith, L. *Nature's Gambit*. New York: Basic Books, 1986.

Hatano, G., Miyake, Y., Binks, M. Performance of expert abacus operators. *Cognition*, 1977, *5*, pp. 47-55.

Simon, H., & Chase, W. Skill in chess. *American Scientist*, 1973, *61*, p. 394-403.

Trotter, R. The mystery of mastery. *Psychology Today*, 1986, *20*, pp. 32-38.

Wiedenbeck, S. Novice/expert differences in programming skills. *International Journal of Man-Machine Studies*, 1985, *23*, pp. 383-390.

IN OUR RIGHT (AND LEFT) MINDS

The notion that we are either right-brained or left-brained has become entrenched in our culture. Actually, it's a pop-psychology myth that the left side of the brain controls only logic and language, while the right side is solely responsible for creativity and intuition. Somehow empirically based, scientific research has been reduced from fact to fiction.

Over the past 400 years, scientific thought surrounding left-brain/right-brain activity has been as split as the brain itself. In the 17th century, the brain was considered to function as a "unified whole." This belief changed as speech centers were discovered in the 1860s. The left side ("half brain") became the

discovered in the 1860s. The left side ("half brain") became the dominant force in our thinking and the focal point of a great deal of research. At that time, the brain's right side was considered unimportant. It was not until 100 years later that this opinion would shift as the result of "split-brain" research. Human existence was believed to be governed by two separate brains — each independent and fully functioning.

Now, it's a different story. Given technological advances and modern research techniques, scientists are back full circle. The 17th century "whole brain" theory may be the correct one after all.

Although brain research started with Hippocrates, it was Rene Descartes, the 17th-century philosopher/scientist/mathematician, who stated that the brain must act as a united whole in order to connect our perceptual world. His whole-brain theory remained the dominant one until the 19th century.

In the 1860s, significant strides in brain research were made. These findings were so pronounced that they changed centuries of theorizing. Paul Broca and Karl Wernicke (French and German neurologists, respectively) reported to the world that damage to the left cerebral hemisphere would produce severe language disorders. They went on to state that comparable damage to the right side did not produce language deficits. As a result, it was obviously the left side of the brain, and not the right, that was essential in daily functioning.

Even though the left and right halves of the brain were similar anatomically, they evidently had very different functions. It was obvious to these 19th-century researchers that language and dominant functions were found in the left side of the brain. As a result, the right side was unimportant. Now, they had a new problem — justifying the existence of the right side of the brain.

To resolve this problem, they concluded that the brain's right side was a nonthinking automation. Therefore, it must be a relay or transfer station for the dominant left side. The right side then took its orders from the left brain. This conclusion was inevitable to these researchers because they already held two important scientific discoveries: 1. The halves of the brain are connected, and 2. The left side of the brain controls the right side of the body and vice versa. Therefore, they concluded that the right brain's use was to inform the left brain what was going on on the side of the body the left hemisphere didn't control, to take commands, and to send messages back and forth to that side. The theory held promise, but it only made half sense. It wasn't until the 1960s that each half of the brain was found to have a mind of its own.

By the 1960s, research took a new turn which would mark the demise of the left brain's reign. Nobel Prize winner Roger W. Sperry and his students were pioneers in their identification of special abilities of the cerebral hemispheres. Thus, we were ushered into the era of "split brain."

Sperry's remarkable findings were the result of his studying individuals who had undergone complete surgical division of the corpus callosum, the connection (or bridge) between the brain's left and right hemispheres. Not common surgery, it was used on these patients as a means of controlling intractable epileptic seizures. When the hemispheres are connected, a disturbance on one side of the brain may spread to the other. Severing the corpus callosum is sometimes used to control seizures, but a pronounced side effect is that the two hemispheres of the brain are now unable to communicate with each other. In the real world, this doesn't cause a major problem, because each side of the brain receives information or experiences from the senses at about the same time; but under laboratory conditions, it was a different story.

Psychologists and neurologists studying this area found that having two independent brains in one body can be quite a dilemma. Because the hemispheres of the brain are not "talking" to each other, it can be a case of the right hand not knowing what the left hand is doing. In fact, there are documented reports of one hand attempting to pull up a person's trousers while the other was trying to pull them down. Or one hand trying to rescue the other hand which did not know how to complete a task, much like another person offering you the answer when you don't know how to solve a problem.

In any case, what Sperry and associates found, using subjects who had undergone split-brain surgery, was that an object placed in the right hand (processed in the left hemisphere; remember that the left side of the brain governs the right side of the body and vice versa) could be identified verbally with no difficulty. But an object placed in the left hand (processed in the right hemisphere) could not be named or described verbally.

Imagine the image of a square flashed to the right brain (nonlanguage center), and a circle being sent to the left (seat of language). If you ask the split-brain person what he saw, he will answer, "Circle." But if you ask him to draw what he saw with the left hand, he will draw a square. Taken a step further, if you flash a naughty picture to the right side of the brain and ask the person what he saw, he will admit to seeing nothing — but with a blush. The examples assume the subjects to be right-handed — 95 percent of all adults use the left side of the brain for speaking, writing, and comprehending language.

The research continued, and by the 1970s, scientists were in agreement that each side of the brain was a highly specialized organ of thought, with one side dominant in a set of skills which complemented those of the other side. The left hemisphere was better at analyzing mathematical problems, judging time and rhythm, understanding and producing language, and coordinating complex movements like those needed for speech. The right hemisphere, once referred to as the minor side because it lacked speech, was superior at perceptual skills; recognition of faces and melodies; expression and emotion; and tasks requiring visualization and manipulo-spatial skills (arranging blocks to match patterns, putting together a puzzle, or drawing a picture). But, somehow, these straightforward findings became garbled, and faulty assumptions arose.

Popular media overpromoted the idea of two brains; one in control when a pianist performs a sonata, and the other in control as a novelist pens a book. If logic were the property of one, then creativity inevitably was the domain of the other. Claims were even made that it was possible to educate one hemisphere at a time. Modern magazines continue to be filled with misinformation about female brains vs. male brains. This is only the beginning of the many left-right brain myths which are alive and well today. Given the popularity of this issue, it's very difficult to separate the facts from the fiction. Here are the facts:

Fact 1. The two hemispheres are significantly similar and are capable of functioning (although imperfectly) even when they are separated by split-brain surgery. This finding has been documented consistently by studying individuals who have undergone split-brain surgery or experienced brain damage as a result of accidents. Remember, split-brain patients with unimpaired senses showed few obvious problems in everyday situations.

Fact 2. Each hemisphere has specialized abilities. It is a widely held belief that each side of the brain has developed specialty areas. There is no doubt that brain regions are differentiated. But, it is not their functioning independently which promotes human behavior. Rather, it is the result of the integration of the abilities, of the two hemispheres working in concert, which creates a special mental procedure, a higher-order process, greater than — and different from — each side's original contribution. The two hemispheres generating ideas, processing each, and stimulating each other, produce more problem solutions than one hemisphere could working in isolation. After all, two heads are better than one; the brain works best as a "unified whole," not one side vs. the other.

Fact 3. The ability to use logic is not an exclusive left-hemisphere property. Just like those individuals who have had left-hemisphere damage, people with right-hemisphere lesions can also exhibit deficits in their logical thinking. There is some evidence that the lack of logic is more pronounced with right-hemisphere damage. For instance, cases have been reported where right-hemisphere-damaged patients will deny that their left arm is their own, or continue to create elaborate plans that are impossible because of an unacknowledged paralysis to the left side. In essence, they are unable to see the logic or lack of logic in their thinking.

Fact 4. Creativity is not exclusively a right-hemisphere function. Creativity most certainly depends on the collaboration of the two hemispheres. Creativity can remain even after damage to the right hemisphere. (For example, after suffering right-hemisphere damage, painter Lovis Corinth still painted with a high level of skill. In fact, some art critics believe that his style was subsequently more expressive than before.)

Fact 5. It is not possible to educate one hemisphere at a time. The reasons are simple. The hemispheres do not function independently, and each hemisphere contributes its special skills to all cognitive processes. Just because the left side is your predominant language center doesn't mean that the right isn't turned in as well.

Fact 6. Although there are differences in the ways men and women process information, these differences tend to be minimal. Researchers admit that some intellectual abilities (hand movements for motor skills and speech production) tend to be more focalized or isolated in women's brains. However, current researchers in this area add two important caveats: 1. Differences at this point tend to be minimal and are overemphasized; and 2. There are likely no inherent characteristics unique to the brains of either sex that limit intellectual achievements of individual men or women.

Fact 7. Even in the most damaged brains, there are vast undamaged areas. This represents the frontier in brain research. The mystery is how to tap into and understand what purpose these unused areas serve. Currently, researchers are attempting to answer these questions as they map the brain and study information-retrieval and storage within the left and right hemispheres of the brain.

On a very positive (and preliminary) note, there is some evidence that the brain is capable of regenerating dead nerve cells. For years, it has been concluded that human beings do not grow more brain cells after birth. Although the research is not yet conclusive, it is promising. This finding will be of such importance that hemispheric differences will become nothing more than an academic question. To be able to regenerate or give new life to damaged areas will restore new meaning and emotional existence to an impaired life.

To summarize, answers to problems are not the exclusive province of one side of the brain or the other. Although there are specialty areas within the brain's two sides, it is the brain's ability to work in concert with itself which creates logical thinking, vivid memories, mathematical prowess, poignant speech, healthy emotions, and creativity.

References:
Kimura, D. Male brain, female brain: The hidden difference. *Psychology Today*, 1985, *19*, pp. 50-58.

Levy, J. Right brain, left brain: Fact or fiction. *Psychology Today,* 1985, *19*, pp. 38-44.

McAuliffe, K. Brain rebirth. *Omni,* 1986, *8*, p. 28.

DAYDREAMS: MORE THAN PIPE DREAMS?

Everyone has the ability to daydream. And, in fact, fantasizing can be a beneficial way of cleaning out those mental cobwebs, and has even been linked to improved mental health.

That parent or third-grade teacher who told you to "stop daydreaming" must not have known about how Mark Twain's dreams of being a pirate, bandit, or trapper-scout were all subliminally achieved in his books. Or mathematician Blaise Pascal, who used daydreaming as a means to alleviate the pain of an excruciating toothache. (And in a fit of painful fantasy discovered the cycloid — the curve generated by a point on the circumference of a circle that rolls on a straight line. But, then, you probably already knew that.) Or Lewis Carroll, who fantasized to minimize migraine headaches and discovered a whole new "wonderland."

Other testimonials to the power of daydreaming prompted complaints during the Spanish Inquisition. Torturers complained that their victims seemed indifferent to pain. Like Pascal or Carroll, the victims visualized pleasant daydreams to distract them from their misery.

Many famous writers have fashioned creativity out of fantasy. Emily Dickinson spent much of her life in isolation, dreaming unattainable dreams, but nevertheless penned over 1,800 poems. Edgar Rice Burroughs used his creative fantasizing to write 28 *Tarzan* books. And Robert Louis Stevenson painted a watercolor map of an imaginary *Treasure Island* on a rainy day in 1881 while entertaining his son.

People who daydream and have an active fantasy life tend to be well-rounded, creative, and more of a pleasure to associate with. What psychologists know is that most people daydream at some point during each day. College classrooms and quiet church sanctuaries are notorious breeding grounds for daydreams. One study found that college students attending a lecture spent nearly one-fourth of the time daydreaming.

Daydreams do not appear to differ between sexes. Although there is a slight bias along traditional sex roles, by and large there is very little difference. Women tend to daydream about personal emotional themes and physical attractiveness. Males, however, tend to focus on more active, athletic, or heroic subjects. But, the "top five" daydream categories are not significantly different for genders. They are: 1. vocational success, 2. romance, 3. money and possessions, 4. achievement, and 5. physical attractiveness.

Additionally, in a daydream one usually chooses sides and becomes either a "conquering hero" or a poor "suffering martyr." As the hero, you are able to leap tall buildings (or employers, family, teachers, and friends) in a single bound. Nothing can harm you. You have all the answers. Impressively — if you do say so yourself — you are invincible. You are perhaps rich, a star athlete, a celebrated actor, famous surgeon, or brilliant lawyer. If your fantasy or daydream is truly grandiose or big-budget, then you are all of the above.

As the suffering martyr, someone has rained on your parade, burst your bubble, or generally made you feel as if you were the lowest of the low, the weakest of the weak, the slowest of the slow, and an overall rotten person. To deal with this turn of fate, you create a daydream which causes that nasty person who made you feel this way to regret his or her actions. It's the old, "they'll miss me when I'm gone, and then they'll be sorry," routine. At this point, you visualize the culprit on bended knee apologizing and begging forgiveness. Of course, martyr that you are, he or she is immediately forgiven.

Although all of us have a choice between being hero or martyr, most people choose the martyr. As a result, two out of three daydreams will be negative ones — that's the pattern. As a result, some people find their daydreams quite distracting.

Daydreaming may be filled with numerous unpleasant emotions like guilt, failure, doubt, and torment.

The same negative scenario is present during sleeping dreams. In fact, 90 percent of all sleeping dreams are negative, and only ten percent are positive. As you know, not everyone remembers his or her nocturnal dreams; but most remember daydreams. Therefore, if you allow it, the negative effects could be rather debilitating emotionally. It's a trade-off. When you actively stop your mind from fantasizing and daydreaming, then you reduce spontaneity and other daydream benefits. Fortunately, most people are happy daydream believers who use fantasies for self-amusement, problem-solving, goal-setting, and future planning.

What are the benefits of daydreaming? First off, daydreams provide a source of stimulation while doing routine or monotonous tasks. For instance, exercise becomes more pleasurable when combined with mental escapes. Now you know why tiny radios and headsets have become so popular; they are a divertisement. In fact, the more repetitive the task, the more likely you are to daydream. Another example would be long, monotonous drives on interstates. There are many times when your mind wanders. All of a sudden you pop back and realize how far you have traveled. Don't panic; fortunately, your brain has a mechanism for monitoring what's happening to you. Even though the daydream has prompted a momentary lapse, it is *not* the same as falling asleep behind the wheel. However, for safety's sake, keep your mind on the road.

Another daydream benefit is in assisting one in delaying immediate pleasures so that future goals become more easily attainable. For example, when you begin a diet, it's inevitable that you become obsessive about food. It really doesn't hurt to daydream about food, providing you keep your hands out of the refrigerator. In fact, fantasizing about food tends to act as a substitute. This was demonstrated during World War II, when subjects volunteered to go on a semistarvation diet for six months. Around the 25th day, their thoughts constantly focused on food. The traditional pin-ups were taken down, and pictures of food became more appealing. If real food is not available to you, then use "mental" junk food. It's much less fattening.

Another interesting aspect of daydream fantasies is that personal aggressiveness can be reduced. For instance, you and a colleague have just had a fight — you even considered punching him or her out. But then you remember the "touch" football game coming up this weekend. As you see yourself asserting your rights as you block that person, you tend to express the hostility in fantasy rather than physically discharging it.

By far the greatest value of fantasy is seen in conjunction with creativity. There is a definite link between a person's ability to fantasize and creativeness. When a person is daydreaming, all is possible. It is quite easy to build the ultimate sports car, write the definitive history of the world, or eradicate the illnesses of mankind. That is, if you will allow yourself to think freely and somewhat childishly.

Robert Louis Stevenson never lost his love for make-believe, nor outgrew his enthusiasm for toys and games. At 17, the Scottish author still enjoyed building houses out of toy bricks, and at 31 invented an elaborate (and addictive) war game, replete with popguns and a full cadre of soldiers. The point here is that he allowed his daydreams to work for him. The most effective daydreams are those which are spontaneous, seem to have "minds" of their own, and are entertaining.

So, with all these wonderful benefits, should daydreaming be encouraged, and perhaps taught? The answer is a resounding "YES." But as every parent and teacher knows, there are limits. Daydreaming is hardly beneficial if you lose touch with the reality around you in the process. If daydreaming and fan-

establish goals. And, believe it or not, fantasies and daydreams are sometimes attainable.

So, when a schoolteacher told you to "stop daydreaming and pay attention," he or she didn't mean it — totally. There is no doubt that discipline is essential; there must be a creative blend which allows for structure and fantasy. Something is shattered when either fantasy is overencouraged, or discipline so rigorous that it doesn't allow appropriate escapes. Never forget that Albert Einstein was a "disorderly dreamer."

To use daydreams and fantasies in a beneficial fashion, visualize your goals. Do something each day to turn your daydreams into realities. If you can see the end-product in your daydreams, then your dream days won't be as far away.

References:
Coon, D. *Introduction to Psychology,* New York: West Publishing Company, 1983.

Madigan, C.O., & Elwood, A. *Brainstorms and Thunderbolts,* New York: Macmillan Publishing Company, 1983.

INTUITIVELY SPEAKING

If you've ever had a hunch that paid off, then you're probably a believer in intuition, or "Executive ESP." If you're afraid to trust your gut feelings and if limited insight forces you to make blind decisions, you're missing out on a most important personal and business management tool. Not only is there evidence that intuition exists, but it may also be the deciding variable which separates the successful businessperson, scholar, or athlete from the average.

Intuition is not a new topic of study. In fact, defining intui-

variable which separates the successful businessperson, scholar, or athlete from the average.

Intuition is not a new topic of study. In fact, defining intuition and determining its origin has intrigued scholars for years. Recently, intuition has been discovered as a "rational alternative." As a result, it's currently a hot topic for personal growth. Even big business, traditionally hard-core analytical, is attempting to rethink and soften its position on "knowledge without basis of fact." However, defining intuition is more difficult than implementing it.

The famous psychoanalyst, Carl Jung, described intuition as one of the four basic psychological functions, along with thinking, feeling, and physiological sensation. Over the years, people have come to explain intuition as the ability to know what to do in a complicated situation without being able to explain why. The intuitive process allows anyone to explore the unknown and to sense possibilities and implications which are not readily apparent. Although it defies the process of rigorous scientific scrutiny, there is evidence that intuition is alive and well.

Intuition is foreign to many, but common in the daily routines of some cultures. The best example is found in Japan. There, a group of professionals use intuition as part of their job description. They are not stargazers or fortunetellers, but hatchery employees. Their job requires them to determine the gender of baby chicks, even though the birds' sexes are indistinguishable shortly after birth. Intuitively, the employees decide which is a rooster or hen with 99-percent accuracy. When questioned concerning their technique of "knowing," they say they have no idea where the knowledge came from or how they did it. They just "know." Even the aspiring apprentices were not sure. The beginners learn the technique by peering over the shoulders of the experienced workers.

The process the Japanese use to separate baby chicks is not a conscious effort. It has been hypothesized that interjecting the conscious element adds confusion and reduces accuracy. Does conscious analyzing interfere and inhibit intuition? This idea was tested under experimental conditions.

One study divided participants into two groups. Each group was presented with an identical list of nonsense words created in accordance with undisclosed, arbitrary grammatical rules. Subjects in the first group were asked to analyze the list and to guess the grammatical guidelines. Those in the second group were required only to memorize the list. Following analysis and/or memorization, all participants were given a new list of nonsense words. Now they were asked which new words matched the rules of grammar implied by the first list. The finding was surprising.

Students who analyzed and consciously tried to create rules were correct less often than those who simply memorized the list and intuitively matched the new list with the old one. Those who analyzed and intellectually sought specific reasons lost sight of the "whole picture." Those who approached the task from a neutral standpoint, simply memorizing words rather than evaluating them, learned more about the synthetic grammar. To them it just seemed "right" that the words in the new list were similar to the nonsense words in the first list. No additional explanation was required.

This does not mean that unconscious, implicit skills are better than conscious, explicit ones, or that right-brain intuitive skills are better than left-brain linear skills. It doesn't follow that analyzing a problem is the wrong approach. The findings suggest that a supposedly unconscious skill, like intuition, complements more conscious skills. In fact, anecdotal research shows that the blending of skills is what makes a good manager a great executive, an average teacher an inspiring one, a physician a healer, or a conscientious employee, creative.

Research has taken a closer look at successful managers. The first finding pointed out that successful senior executives are not locked into the classical/rational mode of problem-solving. In fact, they easily branch out into "softer" approaches like intuition. They somehow know that there's more to management than the cerebral, linear approach of clarifying goals, assessing situations, formulating options, estimating success, making decisions, and, finally, implementing a plan.

Based on information reported in the *Harvard Business Review*, effective managers rely upon a "mix of seasoned intuition and disciplined analysis." To explain, review the following questions:

Which do you prefer — theory or certainty?

What would you rather do — invent or build?

Which is more interesting to you — a concept or a statement?

Which appeal to you more — ideas or facts?

Which do you prefer — figurative or literal explanations?

Which holds more interest — theory or experience?

Which best describes your thinking style — abstract or concrete?

The first word in each pair (theory, invent, concept, etc.) is related to intuitive/right-brain-type answers. The second word (certainty, build, statement, etc.) is indicative of the more cerebral/rational approach. By counting the ones you selected, you can get a rough estimate of your "IQ," or "Intuition Quotient." Count your answers. Were your responses more intuitive or rational?

Almost without exception, top managers in every organization score higher than middle- and lower-level managers on psychometrics designed to measure intuitive traits. The intuitive professional relates well either intuitively or rationally. However, he or she finds theory more appealing than certainty, is more interested in inventing than building, deals more easily with ideas than facts, and has a figurative understanding rather than a constant focus on the literal. He or she is not locked into one style of thinking and processing. Most of all, the individual trusts and implements his or her intuitive skills in several areas.

Senior executives and other successful people fit intuition into their daily routines. It doesn't matter if it's a nine-to-five office-management situation or personal problem-solving; intuition provides a competitive edge over critical analysis alone. It is a powerful tool which can be used for prevention, insight, and a quick check on rational analysis.

First, intuition for prevention. Senior managers can intuitively sense when a problem exists. They use their "hunches" as permission to investigate an isolated fact or event which doesn't seem quite right. With surprising accuracy, intuitive managers usually sense and can uncover problems long before they come to the surface.

Next, intuition provides insight. It is a means by which isolated bits of information and seemingly unrelated experiences are suddenly synthesized into an integrated picture. An intuitive thought can be a flash of insight or a clarifying idea which suddenly surfaces and unifies information which the rational mind would have dismissed as unrelated. Intuition can take one beyond the sum of the parts.

Intuition can also be a check-and-balance on the results of more rational analysis. Each time you hear someone say, "I expected that," or "That's what I thought," he or she has run a problem through an intuitive check. If the rational mind and the intuitive mind agree, it must be the right choice. If, after a rational decision, something undefined is still nagging in your mind, re-evaluate your thinking. Your intuition may be trying to tell you something.

The good news is that intuition is like intelligence — everybody has some. Unfortunately, many of us have "tuned out," "trained out," and dismissed our intuitive skills as unnecessary. Fortunately, it is possible to learn or rediscover dormant intuitive skills.

One of the most effective ways to rediscover or develop intuition is to "What if." That means, instead of taking things as they are, take the opportunity to evaluate by questioning for additional information which can lead to "out-of-the-blue" intuitive discoveries. Start the question with "What if." These two words open up a new realm of possibilities and stimulate your intuitive mind to create new possibilities and alternatives. Don't censor the possibilities; write them down, and put them away for a brief while.

The research on intuition stresses the value of allowing a problem to incubate. In fact, intuition has most often come to scientific investigators when least expected, when normal rational processes were temporarily suspended, and when the press for a solution was removed. Remember the research on analyzers. Too much thinking and rethinking of a problem or situation can deter the intuitive process. Place the problem in suspended animation and allow your own, almost instinctual, abilities to take over. Then, enjoy the flash of insight.

In addition to "What if," four more words are extremely important: "I've seen this before." If something about a problem situation reminds you of a previous experience, listen to yourself and trust your judgment. Recognizing similarities is the first step toward the effective use of intuition. If you just can't put your finger on the similarity, don't press. Back off and give your intuitive mind the space to search, amalgamate, analyze, and incubate.

At the risk of sounding trite, listen to your feelings. An intuitive clue may make its first appearance in consciousness as a twinge of anxiety or a faint glimmer of pleasure. If it just doesn't feel right, don't rush into it. If it feels good and you are ready to trust your intuition, test the issue on a small scale before you commit.

Finally, watch children. They have three skills which provide the foundation for intuition. First, children have a certain spontaneity which allows them to experience and to learn. Second, their beliefs are flexible and fluid. They can suspend judgments. Finally, they have a "mind-set" which is open, receptive, and trusting of new skills. To develop your intuition, try to get in touch with past spontaneity, former flexibility, and the displaced mind-set which gave you permission to explore and to trust your own thoughts and feelings. There are some things which should never be outgrown.

After all, intuition is, as Albert Einstein once noted, "a really valuable thing."

References:

Cosier, R.A., & Alpin, J.C. Intuition and decision-making: Some empirical evidence. *Psychological Reports*, 1982, *51*, pp. 275- 281.

Guillen, M.A. The intuitive edge. *Psychology Today*, 1984, *18*, pp. 68-69.

Isenberg, D.J. How senior managers think. *Harvard Business Reveiw*, 1984, *62*, pp. 80-90.

HOW SOON WE FORGET

Memory is one of those rare human gifts that sometimes goes unnoticed and unappreciated. When it begins to fade, we start expecting the worst. As a result, many false myths have emerged which make the problem worse. They incorrectly explain our ability to forget and retard our ability to remember.

Myth 1: The best memories belong to the intellectually gifted. Not so. The difference is that the gifted have more "memory tricks up their sleeves" than their less-astute peers. There is no doubt that learning potential varies from one person to another, but the ability to remember is inherent in everyone. People with astonishing memories for musical scores, theatrical scripts, chess positions, business transactions, or faces, are everywhere. They are by no means unique.

Myth 2: Good memory is exclusively reserved for the young. False again. In his later years, Arturo Toscanini was noted for his memory. Over the course of his musical career, he memorized every note for every instrument in 250 symphonies and 100 operas.

Although the length of time necessary for a person to retrieve or scan for stored information increases with age, this lag is more likely due to social and health problems rather than the irreversible effects of age.

Myth 3: People have a fixed capacity to remember. Not true. Although this was the prevailing belief in the early 1900s, today's researchers believe that there is no physiological difference at all between the memory of a Toscanini and that of the average person who forgets his car keys or shopping list.

Myth 4: Mentally active people exhibit the same memory decline as their age peers. False. Individuals who flex their mental muscles do not experience the same memory deficits as those who move complacently through this world. In fact, the real difference appears to be that the older person who has an excellent memory has exercised it regularly, and has continually desired to improve it.

Myth 5: Forgetting serves no purpose. False. There are times when either voluntarily or involuntarily "forgetting" something is essential to one's well-being. If an event is too painful, threatening, or embarrassing, it may be forgotten until the person is ready to deal with it. On a day-to-day note, forgetting details actually allows you to sort the trivial from the important. As a result, the brain remains uncluttered with detail. Believe it or not, remembering *too* many sounds, feelings, and sights would make simple understanding quite difficult.

The Dutch scholar Erasmus believed a good memory should be like a fisherman's net. It should keep all the big fish and let the little ones escape. Memory is the same way. Forgetting allows you to reduce things to a manageable size.

Myth 6: Memories decay. False again. There is no limit to the amount of information we can store in our three-pound brains.

Memory is an active system that receives, stores, organizes, alters and retrieves information. If that sounds like computer technology, it is. Although the brain came before the computer, they mirror each other. Of the two, the brain is vastly more reliable and needs only three types of storage compartments: sensory or immediate, short-term, and long-term storage.

Sensory storage is automatic; you really don't have to think about it. It records all sensory stimuli to which one is exposed. These impressions are usually less than a second in duration. They are constantly being replaced with new stimulations. But they are encoded, just like a continuous movie.

Short-term memory is just that — about 30 seconds long on a good day. To measure your short-term memory, calculate how long after dialing you remember a brand-new phone number.

Short-term is where we do most of our thinking. It is a temporary storehouse used for mental arithmetic. To place material in short-term memory, we usually use sounds. That may explain why you repeat a phone number given to you by information either to yourself or out loud before you dial it. Put a person's name in short-term memory, and you'll forget it within half a minute.

What most people don't know is that short-term memory is

Long-term memory is where the past lives. It has two responsibilities: semantic and episodic memory.

Semantic memory deals with such regularly used skills as remembering the seasons, words and languages, months of the year, and days of the week. This type of memory never worries. It really doesn't care when, where, or how you learned the seasons. Episodic memory, however, is autobiographical. Here, everything about life events is recorded. It's not difficult to remember all the facts, senses, or emotions surrounding your first date, first day at college, or your sixth birthday party.

There is one other form of memory, but it is more often forgotten: eidetic imagery or photographic memory. This occurs when a person can scan a lot of information in a short period of time and remember it. This ability is usually seen in children (about eight out of 100); disappears in adolescence; and becomes quite rare during adulthood. Researchers speculate that everyone has photographic memory but that it is traded in for memorization through language as we grow older.

What causes memory changes to take place? There is no definitive answer. Psychobiologists have not located the brain's "memory molecules." But most agree that attention skills, strength of original learning, relevance of material to be remembered, and motivation are crucial factors. There are numerous practical tricks designed to shake out those mental cobwebs. Here are a few.

1. Use mental pictures. Shereshevskii employed a technique known as "loci." When hearing a series of words, he mentally placed them along Gorky Street in Moscow. If one word in the series was "apple," he would, at a precise location on this familiar street, visualize a man dancing on an apple.

2. Read and recite. Those individuals who have the "best" memories spend 20 percent of their time reading and 80 percent reciting what they want to learn — proof that talking to yourself might be a good thing.

3. Avoid unnecessary interference. When new learning conflicts with old learning, the result can be confusion. To resolve this problem, "overlearn" one assignment before beginning another.

Sleeping after memorizing something produces the least interference. If you were somehow placed in suspended animation, time could pass without memory loss. Obviously you can't sleep after every memorization, so plan ample breaks, and practice over a period of days rather than cramming.

4. Memorize the whole thing. It's better to practice and memorize whole parts of information rather than breaking it up into little bits. This is true for short, concise information. To memorize long, complex material, use the progressive part method. First learn a passage marked "A." Then learn parts "A" and "B," then parts "A," "B," and "C," and so on. This is very effective for learning long plays, pieces of music, or poems. Memorizing by this method prevents getting lost and "going blank."

5. Be aware of serial position. This is especially important when things must be memorized in order. You will tend to make most errors in the "middle" of the list. If you meet a lot of people in mid-evening, for example, their names and faces will blur together. When memorizing a shopping list, put the important items at the beginning of the list. As memory fades, the "middle" goes first.

6. Use mental cues. If you're suffering from "tip-of-the-tongue" syndrome, try and recall as many extraneous cues surrounding the memory as possible. For instance, recent graduates can recall about 47 classmates (size of school or class is unrelated). If you've been out of school for 20 years, you can recall 19. To increase this number, take a mental walk down the old school hallway. Remember whose locker belonged to whom. Who sat where in Mr. Reynold's geometry class. Reconstruct mental cues, and new memories follow.

7. Use mnemonics. There are mental systems to aid memory, such as "Thirty days hath September," or the musicians' "Every Good Boy Does Fine" (the notes of the treble clef).

8. Make things meaningful and familiar. Connect new memories with old memories. By forming a chain, you increase the chances of recall. The more bizarre, outlandish, exaggerated, or colorful, the easier they are to remember. This is especially effective in remembering a person's name. For instance, if the name is "Rose," and the person has a bright pink "nose," that's an easy connection. The facial feature triggers the name.

One way to make things meaningful is to create a story using all the objects you want to remember. If you have 100 things to memorize, rote memory will guarantee approximately 28 percent of those. Make up a meaningful story using the objects, and the percentage of things to remember increases to 72 percent. When you give new material a personal reason to be, then you give the memory life.

All a remarkable memory really needs is a little extra attention to detail, a few memory tricks, and a motivation to remember. To summarize, the next time you think your memory's fading, well... put it out of your head!

References:
Luria, A. D. *The Mind of the Mnemonist,* New York: Basic Books, 1958.

Schonfield, D. Memory changes with age. *Nature*, 1965, *28*, p. 912.

Singular, S. A memory for all seasonings. *Psychology Today*, 1982, *16*, pp. 55-63.

Your Behavior is Showing

NASTY HABITS

Allow me to introduce you to "Mr. and Mrs. Behavior Mortifier." They are walking bundles of habits, to say the least. Not the kind that occasionally make their presence known, but the revolting habits which can never be overlooked. They both give new meaning to the third-grade poem, "I have a little shadow which goes in and out with me." When their shadows can't go, it doesn't matter. They still take their bad habits everywhere.

The Mortifiers, collectively, are nailbiting, coughing, denture clicking, hair twirling, scratching, foottapping, jewelry fiddling, bead-bumbling, whistling and gossiping machines. He dots his "i's" with circles; she punctuates hers with tiny daisies. They chew their cuticles, crack their knuckles, pop their chewing gum, and drum incessantly with their fingers.

His passion is sucking on his pen; she prefers to place her writing instrument in her ear. (Nowhere is it written that Bic pens work best when placed in mouth or ear!) Kindly speaking, Mr. and Mrs. Mortifier make "Mr. and Mrs. Whiner" from *Saturday Night Live* look like "Ozzie and Harriet."

But their physical habits don't stop there. They both have equally revolting mental and emotional habits, which are much easier to disguise. He rarely makes it to work on time and never completes his assignments on schedule. His profane language signals his emotional stress, and she constantly worries, which takes wear and tear on her life.

In a restaurant, his spoon-to-plate tapping symphony calls

attention to their overeating. She is known to all of her friends by the affectionate sobriquet of "advice glutton." There has yet to be a problem created for which Mrs. Mortifier cannot offer some innocuous retort. Yet, in all of these annoying antics, they both c ongratulate themselves on their pseudo independence and wide circle of friends. If only they could see themselves as everyone else does...

Habits have the potential to become not only behavior mortifiers, but behavior magnifiers as well. They call attention to you, and their reinforcement feels good. Even negative strokes are better than no strokes at all!

In addition, nervous habits allow you to "turn down the brightness of the day." That means some habits offer an escape from day-to-day worries. For instance, had a fight with your boss? Pretend he's a wad of chewing gum and smack him! Don't know what to say to your superior? Fill in with a few "uhs" and "duhs." Do it often enough, and your habits are showing.

Everybody has bad habits, but few folks actually try to stop them! Everyone acknowledges his desire to stop, but before you know it, nails are being masticated, and the stomach is being distended. Here's how to stop that nasty or generally annoying habit.

1. In the event of multiple bad habits, like Mr. and Mrs. Mortifier, work on one habit at a time. Terminating too many habits all at once is called "setting yourself up to fail." Should you decide to go against this advice, you'll be sorry, because friends will complain that you're a grouch, irritable, and generally no fun. Taking away habits and not replacing them with constructive behavior is painfully boring, provokes feeling of aloneness, and potentially depressing.

Consequently, in order to rid themselves of this new ensuing discontent, most people relapse and start the old habits again. As a result, discomfort for the moment ceases, and maladaptive habits are now etched in stone. Bottom line: Select one habit at a time; extinguish it; and then move on to another.

2. Discover what conditions, times, places, and even people reinforce or reward your habit's persistence. Then, avoid these conditions. For instance, a busy business executive noticed that his one bad habit of talking on the phone was greatly reducing his work output. He didn't realize that his gregariousness was rewarding his inability to complete his duties. Solution: Set aside one particular time of the day for phone calls, have aides screen your calls more carefully, and/or remove the phone.

3. Select a new behavior you've been wanting for years and pair that old, powerful reward with it! So, we say to our busy executive: "Find yourself talking too much and enjoying it less? Too much talking reducing your output? Now's a prime opportunity to join that jogging club, because you can talk all you want while you run." In fact, your favorite behavior of talking will probably make running even more palatable.

4. Narrow cues which elicit that bad habit. Once again, our business executive found himself peripherally watching the push-button phone lines. Each time they were illuminated by an incoming call, his anticipation over "Is this call for me?" required his stopping work. One solution: Put the telephone in your top desk drawer, or work with your back to the phone.

Now about your nasty, disgusting habits. First, decide if you really want to stop. Because if you do, you will; if you don't, you won't. It's as simple as that. For instance, nail-biting (onychophagia) can usually be stopped by recognizing when fingers are being directed toward your mouth and then consistently/immediately putting your hands in pockets, crossing your arms, leaning against something, playing a musical instrument, or any behavior which is incompatible with nail molesting. Always remember: Nails are not considered to have nutritional value.

Do you tug your beard or pull your hair (trichotillomania)? Put a rubber band on your wrist. When your hand goes toward your hair or beard, deliver one painful rubber band pop to your wrist. It doesn't take very long for your brain to catch on! If you're committed, you'll see a sharp decrease in your unwanted behavior by the end of the first day. But don't stop there. Continue to wear your "designer rubber band" until you're satisfied that you've been purged. And don't worry about what others are thinking: chances are you'll start a fashion trend.

One other procedure to stop habits is called "negative practice." Deliberately repeat a bad habit over and over and over until you are totally bored, hurt and/or fatigued by it. This procedure is extreme, but effective. For example, suppose your vocabulary is composed totally of "you knows," "uhs," or "ahs" when confronted with a stressful situation. Take 15 to 20 minutes out of each day for a couple of days and constantly repeat (stopping only to breathe) these distractors. They soon will become very unimportant.

After your old revolting habit has become history and your new behavior is a part of your repertoire, go out and buy that expensive red sports car you've been wanting! You owe it to yourself. Too extravagant? Then select something smaller which allows you to give yourself a gold star or a pat on the back.

Finally, always remember that one nasty habit is worth a thousand words — and none of them is flattering.

References:

Coon, D. *Introduction to Psychology*. New York: West Publishing Company, 1980.

Ferster, C.B., Numberger, J.I., & Levitt, E.B. The control of eating. *Journal of Mathematics*, 1962, *1*, pp. 87-109.

Goldiamond, I. Fluent and nonfluent speech (stuttering): Analysis and operant techniques for control. In M.S. Gazzaniga and E.P. Lovejoy

(Eds.), *Research in Behavior Modification*. Englewood Cliffs, N.J.: Prentice-Hall, 1971.

Mahoney, M.J., & Thoresen, C.E. *Self-Control: Power to the Person*. Monterey, CA: Brooks/Cole Publishing Co., 1974.

Mursell, James L. *How to Make and Break Habits*. New York: J.B. Lippincott Co., 1953.

Perkins, D.G., & Perkins, F.M. *Nailbiting and Cuticle-biting: Kicking the Habit*. Richardson, Texas: Self-Control Press, 1976.

SHYNESS: COYNESS OR COWARDICE?

The lowered eyes, the blushing cheek, the timid pose — what do they really mean? Modest, timid, reticent, bashful, and self- conscious have all been used as synonyms or comparatives for shyness, but in its truest psychological meaning, it simply spells f-e-a-r.

When a friend informs you that he or she is shy, there is a great deal of psychological evidence to support the fact that the person knows (all too well) what shyness is all about. Your shy friend is aware of threatening thoughts and feelings which prompt the heart to pound, the pulse to race, and the face to blush. As a result, he is now embarrassed, which leads to self-consciousness and ultimately, avoidance follows.

If this sounds like you, you're in good company with about 40 percent of the population (four out of every ten people you meet, or approximately 84 million Americans), including notables like Johnny Mathis, Barbara Walters, Robert Young, Roosevelt Grier, Tennessee Williams, and Phyllis Diller.

Researchers have studied shyness at length and still proffer few definitive clues as to its origin. There are those who believe it is inherited, perhaps learned, perhaps a symptom of unconscious rage, or a combination of all of those. What is known is that the term "shy" dates back to 1,000 A.D. when the first use of the word appeared in an Anglo-Saxon poem.

Shyness today means that a person is overly quiet and withdrawn to the point that he suffers from imposed penalties (both internal and external) because he withdraws from what he was supposed or expected to do. Shy people avoid social interactions through verbal hesitations and little or no eye contact. This is a major problem in that the Speech Communication Organization has documented that communication skills (oral and written) are among the most common and expected criteria for promotion.

Psychologically speaking, shyness is a "tendency to avoid social interaction and to fail to participate in social situations."

Here, then, are the facts pertaining to shyness. There is a higher percentage of males (four to one as compared to females) who report being shy. Moreover, our culture tends to penalize males for being shy whereas females are euphemistically referred to as "coy."

The shy person is unable to initiate and structure a conversation. Compared to their non-shy colleagues, they speak less frequently and admit to having more humorous uncomfortable emotions. Furthermore, shy individuals offer fewer affiliative behaviors, e.g., nodding, smiling, gesturing, and gazing.

There are two types of shyness: private and public. In the private type, there is exaggerated sensitivity to inner feelings replete with emotional upset and physiological arousal. The predominant fear revolves around negative or unflattering evaluations of the self.

Borrowed from previous research, the following test will help you evaluate how privately shy you are.

1. I always try to figure myself out.

2. I am overly aware of myself.

3. I reflect about myself too much.

4. I am the subject of my own daydreams.

5. I am overly critical of myself.

7. I am constantly examining my motives.

8. Occasionally I feel that I am off somewhere watching myself.

9. I am very moody.

10. I know how my mind works as I solve a problem.

If you agreed with most of the statements above, your psyche maybe turning on itself. There's nothing wrong with focusing your attention inward, but too much of an egocentric or self-centered focus leads to thoughts and feelings of worthlessness, inferiority and inadequacy.

The publicly shy person sees himself as a "social object." The burden of shyness is greater for this person because he avoids social situations. He is sincerely afraid that he will not respond appropriately. In short, what one does is more important than one's own feelings. Behaving badly to this person is a more egregious error than simply feeling bad.

If you are the public self-conscious type, you will answer "yes" to the following questions:

1. I am concerned about how I do things.

2. I am concerned about how I present myself.

3. I am self-conscious about my appearance.

4. I worry about making the best possible impression.

5. One of the very last things I do daily before leaving for work is to look in the mirror.

6. I am worried about what others think of me.

What makes a person shy? Frankly, your perceptions or thoughts about other people and situations make you shy. In other words, you actually make yourself shy. If you suffer from shyness, then you perceive the following people as those who most often precipitate your shyness: strangers, the opposite sex, authorities (by virtue of knowledge or public role), relatives, elderly people, friends, children, and/or parents. In other words, there is no one safe person in a shy person's eyes.

What situations do you allow to exacerbate your shyness? Most common are large or small groups (especially if you are the focus of attention), social situations, new situations, one-to-one romantic interactions, and vulnerable situations. In short, there is no one safe situation in which the shy person does not fear.

There are ways to conquer shyness, but it must be done one step at a time. People who try to resolve long-standing problems too rapidly are inevitably setting themselves up for failure. In other words, your shyness didn't develop overnight, so be prepared to take time to change.

Although there are numerous how-to books on the market, shyness is difficult to resolve on your own. One very helpful group active in most areas is the Toastmasters Club. They allow for shyness, help you to overcome it, and heighten your self-esteem as well.

Any basic treatment premise involves action. To overcome a shyness barrier, write (and allow yourself to rewrite) "scripts" in advance of social events. Rehearse the script just as an actor would for a performance. Eventually, your stage fright will diminish.

If you have a hard time talking with others, practice on the telephone. Call a local theatre and ask for show times; call a reference librarian and ask for the population of a city or state; call a department store and inquire about advertised products. Pick situations where the people are paid to help you and you can really benefit from the answers. (You'll reduce rejection that way.) Also, be sure to thank the person for the information. The key to overcoming shyness is to reduce ambiguity, or unsureness. All researchers agree that fear of the unknown is a major contributor of shyness.

Add structure to your encounters. Decide in advance where to meet, where to go, what to do before and afterwards, and when to go home. As structure (almost rigid in the very beginning) increases, the "need" for shyness decreases.

To summarize, the shy individual maintains a low profile to avoid intense public or private humiliation. It is a mental handicap which can be as debilitating as some physical infirmities. Shyness is truly one instance when silence is not golden.

In closing, a word to the non-shy: You're lucky.

References:

Carducci, B.J., & Webber, A.W. Shyness as a determinant of interpersonal distance. *Psychological Reports*, 1979, *44*, pp. 1075-1078.

Pilkonis, P.A. Shyness, public and private, and its relationship to other measures of social behavior. *Journal of Personality,* 1977, *45*, pp. 585-595.

Pilkonis, P.A. The behavioral consequences of shyness. *Journal of Personality*, 1977, *45*, pp. 596-611.

Zimbardo, P.G. *Shyness.* Reading, Massachusetts: Addison-Wesley Publishing Company, 1977.

THOSE STAGE-FRIGHT BLUES

Try to imagine the pressure in a business situation where you are standing before a packed boardroom and the outcome of your presentation will determine not only the company's survival, but your own as well. Your reputation is on the line, and you are, in a word, *terrified.* The adrenaline glands shoot energy throughout your body; the heart is beating faster; the hands begin to sweat and shake. Your mind's blank; all thoughts have left your head.

You're not alone. An estimated 80 percent of the population suffers from stage fright, and it can sufficiently limit your career.

Stage fright is not limited to a business setting. Athletes, too, know what it feels like to "choke" when a championship or crucial game is on the line. In 1976, Penn State was facing its second loss in three games. It was fourth down on the Iowa 37-yard line with 50 seconds left to play. Coach Joe Paterno looked to his bench for a kicker. His choice was between two untested players — Matt Bahr (sophomore) and Herb Menhardt (freshman).

Paterno selected Menhardt, who stepped up to give it his best shot. Beaver Stadium was packed with 75,000 fans, all expecting (and demanding) a win. The win was riding on Menhardt's one chance for a field goal. Unfortunately, he hooked the 54-yard kick wide to the left. Iowa scored a 7-6 victory. It would be three years before Menhardt would kick again.

Whether it's a packed boardroom, filled-to-capacity stadium, or standing-room only theatre, there are three elements that predispose a person to choke in that all-important presentation. If you look closely at the boardroom and athletic examples, both have an audience, an unusual level of pressure which leads to heightened self-consciousness, and a chance for personal success. These three ingredients, working in concert, can make a person choke, clutch, panic, and fall victim to stage fright.

Those who suffer from stage fright freely admit that an

audience makes them uncomfortable. Fear of public speaking is so common that it's ranked slightly below death of a loved one and nuclear war in terms of what people dread most.

A great deal of new evidence suggests that an audience can have a devastating effect on a home-team's performance. The research has emerged out of a need to improve team performance in athletic events. For instance, in World Series competitions, home teams make twice as many errors in the final games as they do in the first and second games. The visitors' ability to field improves slightly from the early games to the last.

This negative audience effect has also been tested empirically in the psychologist's lab. Undergraduates were recruited to participate in an experiment which involved deciphering anagrams. One group was privately told that they were expected to do well; the other group was told the same thing by the experimenter, who added extra pressure by staying in the room while they completed the task. When the experimenter, who expected the participant to succeed, stayed in the room watching, the subject exhibited stage fright — and choked.

Another aspect that plays a large part in stage fright is your level of self-consciousness. Interestingly, preadolescent children may be "immune" to choking. In fact, having an audience tends to improve performance up to the age of 12. From then on, self-consciousness takes its toll. Teenagers are especially prone to self-conscious stage fright and choking — even more so than adults.

Self-consciousness is a type of negative thinking. Negative thoughts are linked to dryness in the mouth and rapid heart rates. In situations where individuals became overly self- conscious, approximately 70 percent of their thoughts could be classified as negative. No wonder their performances suffer.

One study tested the relationship between self-consciousness and performance involving three groups of college students participating in a ballgame. One group was told to consciously watch their hands; another was told to focus on the ball; and the final (control) group was given no instructions before trying the game. As one might expect, the group which was told to watch its hands became self-conscious, because the members were paying too much attention to step-by-step motions. To perform most tasks skillfully, one must learn to do them automatically; otherwise, a self-conscious fear of making mistakes takes over. In other words, people who become absorbed in a mechanical, step-by-step execution disrupt the automatic quality of the act. Performance falters.

Of course, psychologists have investigated gender differences as they apply to stage fright and performance. And it would appear that men perceive themselves as having the most to lose. In a party game (really a psychological study), male undergraduates were first tested to see how well they would do. Then they were paired with females (accomplices of the experimenter). The male participants were told one of two things: that, prior to being paired for this task, the females had performed either better or worse than their male partners. In most cases, the men became self-conscious and choked when they believed that the women had done better. Men who were told that the female's performance was below their own did not falter in their abilities. What might have been perceived as an incentive to improve (to avoid being "bested" by a woman) actually prompted self-conscious pressure and lowered performance.

One final point about self-consciousness. People who score high on tests of self-consciousness tend to suffer less from stage fright than those who are typically less self-conscious. Highly self-conscious people apparently cope better with increased self- focus and its pressure. In other words, the less self-conscious you are, the more prone you may be to stage fright.

The third point which is present in most stage-fright cases is called "redefinition of identity" by psychologists, or a chance for personal success and acclaim. In other words, winning a championship is the highest goal of most athletes. An executive who lands a multimillion-dollar account now has the ability to leap up the corporate ladder rather than one step at a time. That one account or one extra point allows you to stand out like a star. A situation that allows the opportunity to favorably redefine your identity causes pressure and stress. But, if you pull it off, you're a celebrity, the boy/girl genius, the expert.

Identity can be redefined positively. In 1976, when Menhardt choked on the crucial field goal, it took specialized training to emotionally prepare him for his second chance. In November 1979, Menhardt was called upon to make a last-second, 54-yard field goal in a game against North Carolina State. He succeeded, and Penn State won, 9-6.

From the boardroom to the classroom to athletic competition, 95 percent of all stage-fright victims can be treated successfully. Here's how:

The first aspect involves learning how to organize your thoughts. If there's order in your head, it's much easier to translate it to an audience. Never be afraid of an index card; organize your plan of attack on paper and refer to it during the presentation.

In addition to organizing your thoughts, effective body language also gives that extra boost of confidence. Learn how to stand, and how to make appropriate gestures. Plant your feet squarely, scan the room, offer eye contact, and take charge.

Relaxation skills are essential in keeping anxiety in check and positive thoughts flowing freely. If anxiety is allowed to spiral, stage fright will take over. Focus on slow, rhythmic breathing. If you find that you don't know how to relax and anxiety continues to swell, some professional assistance may be in order to help resolve the problem.

Finally: practice, practice, practice. Although some professionals believe that stage fright and choking may be due to shyness, there is also evidence that suggests it's simply due to lack of experience. Practice your speech in front of a mirror; try it out on friends. Check around for short courses in public speaking.

Remember, stage fright is a common problem. When you're faced with a situation where you will be watched, evaluated, and allowed no second chance, don't panic. Overprepare and give it your best shot. Then move on to the next opportunity.

References

Baumeister. R.F., The championship choke. *Psychology Today,* 1985, *49,* pp.48-52.

Galassi, J.P., Frierson, H.T., & Sharer, R. Behavior of high, moderate, and low test anxious students during an actual test situation. *Journal of Consulting and Clinical Psychology*, 1981, *49*, pp. 51-69.

Mereson, A., When all eyes are on you. *Science Digest,* 1985, *93,* p.21.

Stark, E., Pretty scary, huh? *Psychology Today*, 1985, *49,* p.16.

THE GREEN-EYED MONSTER

Jealousy is no stranger to the human emotional spectrum, but its intensity varies from individual to individual. In fact, it is so pervasive that jealousy has been given many names, among them, erotomania, psychose passionelle, Othello Syndrome, green-eyed monster, mark of Cain, and the dragon in paradise. In addition, jealousy has a well-deserved listing as one of the Seven Deadly Sins, because once it invades, destruction follows.

Where does jealousy begin? It starts as early as one preschooler saying to another, "My dog's better than yours."

However, it is hardly limited to kiddie rivalries, and can be disguised in a thousand shapes.

Jealousy flashes its green eyes when one employee envies a co-worker's extra privileges (refusing to see that fringe benefits must be earned); when a lonely person's bitterness is projected to a popular peer (denying his own inadequacies as a cause of envy), or when one nation is belligerent towards another (in the name of peace).

Jealous comparisons occur with extraordinary frequency. Alfred Adler, the Viennese psychologist, explained that, "All problems (of which jealousy is a type) are social problems in a social setting, and there are no other problems."

To clarify, when two people meet, discord may follow, particularly if one of the dyad views himself as a second-class citizen. As a result, jealousy is a symptom covering up one's own perceived inadequacies and thoughts of inferiority.

If unresolved, jealousy becomes an overall condition whereby a person destroys himself from the inside out. It is childishly self-centered and produces self-pity, oversensitivity, psychosomatic or body ailments, dependency and envy.

It is important to distinguish envy from jealousy. Although there are many similarities, there is a difference. Simply put, envy is the desire to acquire another's possession, i.e., keeping up with the Joneses, while jealousy is the fear of losing a current "possession," and is concerned with the "overmaintenance of a relationship."

The two — jealousy and envy — working together become a vicious cycle, or, in computer jargon, an infinite loop from which there is no exit. The emotional response is irrational because jealousy reinforces envy and vice versa. One prompts the other, and both get blown out of proportion. As Shakespeare's Othello put it, "Tis a monster/Begot upon itself, born on itself."

Although most people tend to think of jealousy as a by-product of a love relationship, the green-eyed monster is seen in all spheres of human relations. However, as business environments tend to promote competition, a logical side effect is jealousy, readily found among the work force. In other words, the green- eyed monster may wear a three-piece suit.

In a business setting, jealousy diverts and destroys collective energies. Instead of a group working for a common or superordinate goal, gratification of individual needs becomes the focal point. The industry's priorities are reduced to second place. In order to achieve jealousy-obsessed individual goals, to assert one's claim, and to ultimately win over another, jealous exploitation may resort to lying and cheating.

Of all types, shapes and varieties of jealousy, its prime mover is self-pity. One can always find another who appears to be more materially affluent or more intellectually astute. By dwelling on another's possessions versus one's own shortcomings, self-pity and hypersensitivity emerge. In order to reduce resulting malcontent, a plan of action born of jealousy is created. These jealous planners fit the following categories: the Martyr, the Overcompetitor, the Tyrant, and the Motivator.

The jealous Martyr enjoys the pain of jealousy for suffering's sake. Such people use jealousy to put themselves down before others get the opportunity. They are intimidated by everyone they meet, and are convinced the rest of the world is better off than they are. They choose to do nothing about their condition. They become martyrs enjoying "halo pressure." These victims are unproductive, and never resolve their jealousy.

Because he sees himself as champion and hero, the Overcompetitor bottles up his jealousy and rarely deals with his self-pity overtly. The slightest inequality is interpreted as permission to battle. The most minor infraction now becomes an instrument of war. Always remember, in his own mind, the Overcompetitor never loses. His plan is always victorious.

Viciousness separates the Overcompetitor from the jealous Tyrant. This green-eyed monster is venomous. Antisocial behaviors (e.g., lying, cheating, etc.) are used to control others. Any means is available to justify his possessive ends. He must control all that he touches, and he rarely feels guilt.

Unlike the other jealous planners, the Motivator uses his fear of loss and hypersensitivity skills as an agent for positive change. He understands that life's problems demand independent solutions; he recognizes "cooperative competition." To this person, jealousy is an alert signaling a threat to personal security; however, it does not threaten his identity. As a result, his emotions are not clouded, and he is capable of developing a strategy to resolve a perceived loss.

The procedure to resolve jealousy first demands a clear understanding of the condition's symptoms. First, the reaction looks childish and imitative. The jealous person is overly sensitive, acts as if secret wishes are binding on others, and is unable to tend to his own affairs. As a result, he demands special favors. Finally, in his heart of hearts, he is very lonely. This clinical description holds for the paranoid executive as well as the star-crossed lover.

Not surprisingly, men and women tend to express their jealousy (and their envy) differently. Males are more likely to express anger, projecting their dislike onto the world. This anger is, of course, a cover-up and protects the culturally defined "masculine pride."

Females, on the other hand, are more likely to assume fault and turn their anger on themselves. Fortunately, this stereotypic response is changing, and a greater number of females are confronting this problem directly.

How does one manage the greed, selfishness and insecurity of jealousy? To paraphrase, how does one tame the green-eyed monster?

First, recognize that jealousy is a signal or a warning. It becomes devastating when you decide to wallow in it and avoid a plan of action. Next, decide whether you are reacting to a true loss or simply an alleged threat. Your brain sets up an "appropriate" emotion depending on what you tell it. If you decide that the threat is legitimate, give the other party an explicit communication of expectations. Such a communication is risky, so be prepared to take hold lightly and to let go just as lightly. Such a tactic frees you from jealous dependency. Finally, jealousy "workshops" are springing up all over the country. Perhaps a small investment of time and dollars is justified if your jealousy is debilitating.

Jealousy is common because most people respond like children longing to be loved. By the same reasoning, the surest way to conquer the green-eyed monster is to master the art of unselfish loving.

References:
Beechers, M., & Beecher, W. *The Mark of Cain: An Anatomy of Jealousy.* New York: Harper & Row, 1971.

Clanton, G., & Smith, L. *Jealousy.* Englewood Cliffs, New Jersey: Prentice-Hall, Inc., 1977.

Schoenfield, E., *Jealousy: Taming of the Green-eyed Monster.* New York: Holt, Rinehart and Winston, 1979.

Silver, M., & Sabini, J. The perception of envy. *Social Psychology,* 1978, *41,* pp. 105-117.

PERFECTION: IMPOSSIBLE DREAM?

Over the years, most of us have come to believe that only perfectionists succeed. After all, these superachievers are lauded for their attention to detail, follow-through, and overall concern for meticulousness in all areas of their lives — both personal and professional. However, the quest for the best has serious side effects and may be causing more problems than successes. There is evidence that it may not be worth it to be perfect — at least not all of the time.

Simply put, a perfectionist is someone whose achievement level has gone awry. He or she strains compulsively toward improbable goals, basing self-worth on achievements. As a result, errors and mistakes terrorize them. When they do succeed, it is not enough. They must do better. They are driven, but unable to really enjoy their accomplishments.

The sad news is that researchers estimate that this problem is increasing. In fact, one study estimated that as many as 40 percent of the salespeople surveyed experienced problems in this area. Though there's no doubt that a healthy search for excellence is necessary to get through life, textbook perfectionists are out of control and unable to break out of this cyclical "trap."

Psychologists agree that this trap is primarily a mental one. In fact, the reason is simple. Perfectionists are controlled by one dominating, imperfect thought.

Perfectionists believe that total success or ultimate perfection is within their grasp if they just work hard enough. Unfortunately, they set themselves up to fail, because they cannot see that they are placing their own standards further and further away from realistic reach. The harder they try, the more they fail. The result is a vicious cycle of self-defeat and limited productivity. This finding has been demonstrated not only in the laboratory but also in real life.

In a recent study, insurance agents were given a questionnaire which measured their perfectionist thoughts. The plan was to compare their level of perfectionism with sales performance. Common sense would suggest that those with perfectionistic standards would also have high sales levels. The results did not support this assumption.

The average earnings among the two groups were significantly different. The perfectionist group tended to average $15,000 a year less than their nonperfectionist colleagues.

The same results were also found in another study. The participants were not salespeople, but male gymnasts. Two groups of gymnasts were surveyed: Olympic qualifiers and non-qualifiers. When perfectionistic attitudes were surveyed, results turned out to be the same as those found in the insurance study.

The Olympic qualifiers did differ from those who were not selected. Ability notwithstanding, the Olympic athletes did not dwell on past failures. Those athletes who did not qualify were likely to "psyche themselves out" almost to the state of near panic. The nonqualifying group was more likely to set unreasonable perfectionistic standards and have greater difficulty recovering from mistakes. The result was poorer performance, self-doubt, and failure.

From these two studies, the cultural myth that perfectionists are more productive is clearly false. The inability to meet goals is only one problem. There are other, even more serious, side effects.

Although the perfectionist is less productive, there are three areas in which he does win out over his nonperfectionistic peers. These are 1. loneliness/relationship problems; 2. limited self- acceptance; and 3. moodiness.

The first of these, loneliness, stems from the perfectionist's obvious fear of making mistakes — or, to put it more succinctly, of looking silly or foolish. It's easy to see that the perfectionist often anticipates rejection. To prepare for it, he or she reacts defensively, by using criticism. Because they believe that their foibles will not be accepted by others, perfectionists try and push you away before you recognize their inadequacies. As a result, they do not easily self-disclose with others. The result is loneliness and relationship problems.

Concerning self-acceptance, the true perfectionist is quite unforgiving. He sees himself as an enemy, and the more he fails to meet self-imposed goals, the more convinced he becomes of his inadequacies. He is unable to accept himself for what he really is. This area was tested at the university level, and the results support that perfectionistic thinking leads to decreased self-acceptance.

Participants completed three tests in the following areas: self- acceptance, depression, locus of control, and perfectionism. Although the study was a correlational one and did not imply causality, the researchers did find that self-acceptance was negatively related to depression, externality, and perfectionism. In other words, the person who accepted himself and his abilities was not likely to test out as depressed. Additionally, he saw himself as master and in control of his life (externality). Finally, with high self-acceptance, a person is less perfectionistic and able to allow himself to make mistakes.

Those students with low levels of self-acceptance were likely to be moody or depressed, to feel controlled by outside forces, and to exhibit the desire to be perfect in word and deed. Perfectionism tends to be linked in a vicious cycle with limited self-acceptance, loss of control, and mood disorders.

Concerning moodiness and depression, it is not unusual for the textbook perfectionist to feel performance anxiety, stress, and anger quite poignantly. His imperfect thoughts suggest that pushing harder is the way to get rid of these feelings. This exacerbates the situation. Over-zealous, irrational pushing is causing the problems. To that point, a study of 105 undergraduates found a direct relationship between mood and perfectionistic thinking.

These university students were given a depression inventory and perfectionism scale. A relationship was found between depressed mood and perfection. Using regressive analyses, the researchers concluded that current desires for perfectionism can be linked to later depression. But good news also came out of this study.

It was found that perfectionism early in life and later resolved did not predict future depression. In other words, learning how to deal with a desire for perfection decreases the probability of future emotional disorders, specifically depression.

Fortunately, there are ways to deal with perfectionism, and it starts in your own mind:

1. Learn how to mentally "filter" your thoughts. Perfectionists tend to focus on all the bad things which have happened to them and discount successes as if they never happened. Carry a note pad, and for the next several days jot down all the things you accomplish successfully. When you begin to dwell on negative things, take out the book and read about your recent successes.

2. Evaluate your current standards. To do this, psychologists suggest that you compare yourself to a set criteria. Ask your colleagues at work what they are working for, what constitutes a success, and at what point they walk away from an uncompleted assignment. Write down their answers; then ask your employer the same questions. Write down his or her answers. Finally, ask your husband or wife. Now you have three different perspectives or criteria on which to base your new standards.

3. Celebrate your successes. This is an excellent way to deal with the loneliness so characteristic of perfectionism. Everyone likes to party and have fun. So, encourage some of your friends to go out and celebrate even the smallest success with you (and your family). If you don't have a success story to celebrate, make one up. The point here is to reinforce yourself for a job well done and to counter those negative, nagging "you-can-do- better" thoughts.

4. Learn from your mistakes. When you err — and you will

— ask yourself what you would do differently in a similar situation. Visually see yourself responding in a new, more effective way. By doing this, you store the new scenario in your memory and begin to counteract negative thinking. This is an effective thought-stopping technique. When a nagging thought or previous failure pops in your head, rewrite and visualize a mental action, and give it a happy ending. Then, every time you think about the bad situation, substitute the visual thought which has a happier, more positive finale.

5. "Practice" mistake-making. Pick some innocuous situation and make a mistake. Perhaps you call a person by a wrong name. Allow him or her to correct you, smile, and say to yourself. "That didn't hurt as much as I thought it would." The point here is that perfectionists think that mistakes are extremely painful. Most are not.

6. List the advantages and disadvantages of being a perfectionist. You will find that the cons far outweigh the pros. Post the list in a conspicuous place so that you get the message regularly and often.

7. Finally, and most importantly, take a good look at your current level of self-acceptance. To raise your current self-regard, give yourself permission to make mistakes; surround yourself with positive situations which give you a lift; and, most importantly, find someone with whom you can be honest and open. Then explain your fears and worries. If you feel that you are not at a place where you can talk with a person freely, use a journal or dictate to yourself as you go to work. The point is to get the problem out of your head and on the table. This reduces internal pressures tremendously.

Fortunately, there's a seed of healthy perfectionism in everyone. It serves as that special quality which pushes us to achieve. Unfortunately, some allow the desire for perfection to grow out of control. Then, instead of functioning as a motivational push, it keeps the person going round and round in circles of unproductivity. Be willing to settle instead for being almost perfect.

References:
Burns, D. The perfectionist's script for self-defeat. *Psychology Today,* 1980, *15*, pp. 34-52.

Hewitt, P.L., & Dyck, D.G. Perfectionism, stress, and vulnerability to depression. *Cognitive Therapy & Research*, 1986, *10*, pp. 137-142.

Mihalik, M. A perfect way to be miserable. *Prevention,* 1986, *38*, pp. 50-54.

Pirot, M. The pathological thought and dynamics of the perfectionist. *Individual Psychology: Journal of Adlerian Theory, Research & Practice,* 1986, *42*, pp. 51-58.

ON THE DEFENSIVE

Imagine how psychologically devastating it would be if all of your beliefs and attitudes were suddenly stripped away, and you had to encounter the "real" you. Or imagine the trauma of being forced to view the world as it really is — no fantasy, no daydreams for escape, no way to protect or insulate yourself from present, past, or future hurt.

Fortunately, our psyches have ways of protecting us from potential harm. It may be as simple as turning away from an unpleasant sight, refusing to discuss distasteful topics, becoming preoccupied with work, or even fainting when confronted with a difficult situation. Any one of these actions can shield, or mask, the real problem so that it is briefly out of sight and out of mind. These coping behaviors, essential for effective day-to-day living, are called defense mechanisms.

Defense mechanisms are reactions people undergo when they think that they are being attacked or criticized. They are generated within the mind to protect the ego from "system overload." Simply put, a defense mechanism is a psychological cushion which insulates the hard truth from your awareness until time can soften the pain. They emerge as an attempt to cope with our contemporary world's frenetic pace and problems. As a result, they are the necessary glue which holds personalities intact and prevents emotional breakdowns.

Everyone is a walking bundle of defense mechanisms. They allow us to maintain a positive, almost idealized self-image so that we can comfortably live with the good and bad within ourselves. These mechanisms protect us, but should be used with care.

Freud was the first to use the term "defense mechanism." He chose this expression because he wanted to keep up with the trend of the day. In the early 1900s, it was fashionable to think of human functions in machine-like ways.

Today, due to the impact of computers, mental-health professionals view the same Freudian idea in terms of information processing. To that point, a defense mechanism manipulates your level of awareness concerning specific information, facts, events, and people. As a result, the "real" situation can be denied, distorted, or even restricted from your awareness. When this happens, emotion and self-involvement are reduced. Finally, the potential threat, damage, or harm is counteracted and rendered harmless. Defense mechanisms are designed to do one thing: to reduce potential discomfort, anxiety, and/or frustration. They buy time.

As you would expect, there's a hierarchy of potential defense mechanisms. Some are very simple and easy to spot; others are more complicated, sophisticated — and are powerful deceivers. However, the most common and least effective defense mechanism of all is anger.

No matter how you look at it, anger is a cover-up. It's not even a primary emotion. In fact, it is considered a secondary one, because the temper masks what is really going on inside. In other words, the aggressive action manifested through anger is saying, "I'll get you before you get me!" The anger is used to intimidate the other person so that he or she will never again try to inflict harm on you.

If, somehow, we could look past a person's anger and see what's really going on, chances are we would find that anger belies hurt, anxiety, and worry. But why is anger so common and so easily allowed to emerge? It is socially accepted and considered a sign of strength. Only "wimps" show their true feelings — or so our culture believes.

The next time your temper flares, stop and ask yourself: "Why am I so defensive? What am I covering up?" and "Is there another way to handle this problem?" It is wise to avoid aggression as a means of dealing with difficulties. Any time anger emerges, it tends to heighten, rather than reduce, conflict. The person to whom the anger is directed now has a desire to retaliate rather than deal with his or her own hurt feelings.

Another very common defense mechanism is denial. Management finds it impossible to believe that it is responsible for the company's going bankrupt. One partner in a marriage is "always the last to know" that a divorce is imminent. An extremely stingy person denies that he is a tightwad. These blind spots are everywhere. By lying to ourselves, we avoid, deny, or distort the truth until we work up the courage to deal with the situation.

Denial is not the only trick we use to soften reality. Through rationalization, we justify our actions to ourselves and others. As a result, we manufacture faulty logic which allows us to do what we know we shouldn't.

Erich Fromm, the famous psychoanalyst, put it best when he said, "However unreasonable or immoral an action may be, man has the insuperable urge to rationalize it — that is, to prove to himself and to others that his action is determined by reason, common sense, or at least conventional morality." In other words, we make excuses so that our failures won't look as catastrophic.

Having trouble with your sales quota? Unable to manage effectively? Not doing well in your work? The magnitude of these types of problems would be overwhelming without a defense mechanism or two to protect your fragile ego. To deal with these worries, a rationalized excuse might be, "I refuse to get involved in the competitive rat race!" As a result of your taking *any* stand (it doesn't matter if it's right or wrong), you spare yourself humiliation and total defeat. Even if you're fired, rationalization will help you create a reason why it's not your fault.

The two most common forms of rationalization are "sour grapes" and "sweet lemons." Sour grapes is the technique we use to make an unobtainable goal seem less appealing. For instance, if you were not invited to a party, you might tell yourself, "I really don't want to go. It's probably going to be pretty dull." Of course, deep down you know that the evening's activities will probably be the social event of the season, but, at least for the time being, your ego has been spared rejection.

Sweet lemons is when you convince yourself that an undesirable situation is really positive. How do you deal with the fact that you were ripped off thousands of dollars for a gas-guzzling automobile, accepted an undesirable job, or spent hundreds of dollars beyond your means (just to keep up with your neighbors)? You claim the sleek, aerodynamic design makes up for the gas- guzzling problem; the potential future advancement and ultimate salary softens the daily routine of a boring, undesirable job; and the fact that your family deserves the best justifies the discomfort of being over-extended. These "good points" (excuses) attempt to lessen anxiety and help to defend your mistakes.

There is one other use of rationalization, and it's called the "I-was-only-trying-to-help" syndrome. For instance, your boss catches you rummaging through an off-limits file cabinet. Rather than admit that you're doing something wrong, you immediately say, "Yes, I thought you might want to see this." The next time you make a mistake, you rationalize and say, "I'm sorry. I was only trying to help." At least, in your mind, you're still a good guy. How can they hate someone who was only trying to help?

It's clear that fate, bad luck, chance, and destiny are overworked when it comes to explaining failure. That's another defense mechanism in operation — projection. This it's-not-my-fault syndrome allows us to transfer blame. A delinquent child blames his parents. An athlete attributes defeat to the referee. Two children caught fighting claim that "he hit first." The student who failed the examination blames the teacher. The manager who didn't meet quota accuses his staff.

Projection is turning the spotlight of failure away from you and pointing it at someone else. It doesn't matter whom you hurt. To shift responsibility is a human trait, although not a very adult one.

There is one defense mechanism which is impressive and offers hope for success. Known as compensation, it allows you to change the focus of, or to cover up, one weakness by emphasizing a more positive ability within your own life.

For instance, Franklin D. Roosevelt's outstanding achievements in politics followed his being stricken with polio. His political acumen significantly overshadowed his physical condition. Charles Atlas made a successful career out of bodybuilding in spite of the fact that he was a frail and sickly child. Helen Keller, unable to see or hear, emphasized her abilities as a thinker and writer rather than dwelling on her physical weaknesses.

The point here is that the best way to deal with a negative is by using a positive. That's good advice for any situation.

There's no need to lie to yourself when a positive truth will work just as well.

There are many other defense mechanisms which have been identified over the years. They all do the same thing. They protect us from "the slings and arrows of outrageous fortune." Everyone uses defense mechanisms to a degree. They are certainly necessary for day-to-day living. But too much of anything can create obstacles.

If your friends are constantly prefacing their remarks to you with "Now, don't get defensive," and if you are always the last to know, take a good look at how effectively you're dealing with problems. If things are *never* your fault, chances are your defense mechanisms are working overtime.

References:
Freud, A. *Ego and the Mechanism of Defense* (Revised Edition), International Universities Press, 1967.

Fromm, E. *The Sane Society*, New York: Holt, Rinehart, & Winston, 1955.

MY MISTAKE!

Everyone realizes that there is no way to completely avoid errors, but at no time in our history has the potential impact of mistakes held such powerful sway. As a result, a new term has emerged — "techno-error," and it denotes any oversight in our high-tech age which, if handled improperly, leads to serious consequences. Fortunately, techniques to minimize the impact of techno-errors are being identified.

Our view of mistake-making has changed with the times. Modern computing methods, increased competition, information processing, and the emergence of sophisticated high-tech devices have forced scientists (and big business) to view the simple mistake in a different light. As a result, the psychological focus is to develop approaches which minimize errors and maximize their correction.

When Sigmund Freud promoted his ideas about errors and unconscious thinking, he did so in a much simpler era. However, he did suggest that something, either consciously or subconsciously, interferes with a person's ability to act. This simple point has led psychologists to study how stray information seems to overpower, influence, and cause error. They have now categorized common mistakes, documented specific ways the brain seems to trip itself, identified human behaviors associated with mistakes, and tested techniques which reduce an error's impact. From corporate functions to family gatherings, these ideas have wide applicability.

Overall, there appear to be three general types of mistakes: "assumption," "selection," and "capture" (the most common).

An assumption error occurs when a person is so caught up in descriptive details that he or she fails to notice, or misinterprets, an essential piece of information. The individual assumes everything is in place, plans accordingly, and overlooks a critical point. The work is performed incorrectly until this one piece (totally unexpected, yet obvious all along) is identified and brought to one's conscious attention.

An excellent example follows in the childhood riddle: "Railroad crossing look out for the cars, see if you can spell 'it' without any 'r's." The point is that one gets caught up in the rhetoric of railroads and cars and fails to see that the person is asking you to spell the word "it" without using the letter "r."

In the corporate environment, assumption errors are common. For instance, memorandums and directives, similar to routine policy but with minute changes, may never be followed. Employees may think they have seen the same paperwork before, and consequently read past or overlook the new points.

The second common mistake is usually one of selection. Imagine the harried clerical person rushing to send out two overnight proposals. The contents are clearly marked; yet somehow, the parcels are accidentally switched. Although the worker undoubtedly knew which package went where, a selection error transpired. These mistakes tend to occur when a person is tired or under stress. For instance, someone who is planning a party makes a selection error when the cake is put in the refrigerator and the salad is stored in the oven. In both examples, the person knows what to do, but makes the wrong selection.

The final type is the most common and is called a capture error. The reasoning is simple: a more powerful habit or behavior captures your attention and causes you to make a mistake. In other words, if, while working on one project, you pass too near a well-formed, stronger habit, it will reach out and "grab" you. Mentally, you're thrown off track, and your behavior conforms to the better-formed habit.

Say you are searching for a lost item and decide that it's in your office; however, something else captures your attention as you move into the office. Now that you are in there, you've suddenly forgotten what you're looking for. The reason: your office "captured" you. All of your thoughts surrounding work take precedence over the lost object. There you stand, wondering *why* you came into your office, and it may take a few moments for you to remember what's going on after your thoughts have been captured.

There are five mental patterns which can lead to errors. They are the result of perseveration, preoccupation, indecision, short-term memory overload, and one-way internal models or plans.

Perseveration is a big word which simply translates into stubbornness. Errors are made because a person has made a decision and refuses to change it even when new evidence is presented. More importantly, this new evidence clearly indicates that the person made the wrong decision, but he or she stubbornly refuses to change as a result of it. Ego is obviously involved in this type of error.

The next processing procedure which leads to error is called preoccupation or fixation. Here, the person on a project becomes so involved with one (albeit trivial) aspect that more important tasks are completely overlooked. In other words, the person becomes so absorbed by one minor detail that he or she can no longer see the big picture. The result is error.

The third type of processing error results from indecision, or as psychologists call it, alternation. Simply put, the decision-maker vacillates, changing his or her mind all too frequently. The decision continues to change from one moment to the next — without reason. The important point is that there is no basis for the continued change. Indecisiveness occurs even when the facts of the case remain constant. The person acts as if he or she were gambling. At some point, he or she will make the correct decision, which fortutiously occurs at the right moment.

Short-term memory overload is very common, especially in those work situations where a person is required to juggle a lot of information. In other words, if there is a great deal of data coming in, the brain can only store so much in its short-term memory. If there is no room left to store, then the brain does not discriminate. Important information is discarded just as easily as nonessential data. The result is a processing error due to sensory overload. People who say, "I've got too much on my mind," are telling you that they are prone to error.

Finally, one-way internal modeling is a type of inadequate planning. Most everyone understands and creates memory designs which relate to personal or professional functioning on a daily basis. However, when an emergency hits or some mistake which is totally out of the ordinary transpires, current memory does not serve very well. When a mistake or accident takes place for which there is no prior basis of understanding or planning, we still tend to rely on models or prior learning stored in our memories.

Unfortunately, prior learning has no basis in this reality; it is a totally new experience and has never happened before. As a result, when you actualize what you have learned to do in the past, the end product is likely greater error in this new, abnormal situation. To reduce the impact of this type of error, prior planning and rehearsal for even the least exigency is essential.

Sometimes there is very little one can do to stop an error in its tracks. However, how one handles the mistake is integrally linked with minimizing an error's impact. When an error is handled correctly, one earns a stronger reputation. If a mistake is handled incorrectly, it can be devastating and more memorable than the error itself. Of course, psychologists have identified possible approaches to handling mistakes. Some work, and some don't.

Probably the most typical way to deal with a mistake is to refuse to acknowledge that it ever happened. People will use denial and hope that no one notices — wishing the mistake will just go away. In fact, the longer one delays, the more it can haunt one.

Another way to handle mistakes is to shift blame. People who do this are so caught up in preserving their identities that they probably have little worthwhile identity to preserve. It is not unusual for this type of person to lie, bluff, or withhold portions of the truth from superiors. A side effect of this approach is that they alienate others. Simply put, this person is unable to admit his or her mistakes and prefers to blame others for everything — another dishonest and ineffective approach.

Then there are those who are so honest and concerned that they overapologize. At first, the concern is genuine; but after a time of constant apologizing, the impact is lost. The problem here is that the person has honestly accepted blame, but is now wallowing in sorrow for an extended period of time, and not attempting to solve the problem. As a result, he or she comes across as ineffective and inept.

Finally, there is the overanalyzer. When a mistake occurs, this person immediately starts searching for all the good reasons why it happened. Constant rationalizers, they are so busy justifying the mistake that no one learns how to resolve the problem, or stop it from occurring again.

How should one handle mistakes? It is a four-step process. Consider the following survey.

A recent study evaluated 20 successful Fortune 500 executives and a corresponding group of 20 executives whose careers had been sidetracked. The study found that one major difference between the two groups was the ability to handle mistakes. The successful executives knew that it was impossible for them to perform perfectly all the time, and they were secure in admitting their fallibility. Moreover, of the successful executives surveyed, a common four-step strategy for dealing with errors emerged.

When a mistake is made, openly accept responsibility. State your regrets for any inconveniences, but avoid the word "sorry," as well as overemphasizing the mistake.

Immediately notify anyone who may be affected by the error. Clients and coworkers will treat you with more respect when warned in advance. It is important that you inform them of what they may expect and perhaps provide a plan of action.

Create a solution(s) which will resolve the mistake and immediately implement that strategy.

Analyze the mistake, evaluate the solution's effectiveness, learn from the situation, and put it away. Successful executives did not dwell on their errors. It was back to business, as usual.

Finally, never be afraid of mistakes. They only become a problem when you run out of solutions.

References:
Mambrino, E. To err is devine. *Success*, 1986, *33*, p. 26.

Norman, D.A. Why people make mistakes. *Reader's Digest*, 1980, *117*, pp. 103-106.

Wolkomir, R. Techno-error. *Omni*, January 1984, *6*, p. 30ff.

THOSE BIG "0" BIRTHDAYS

Is there life after 30, 40, 50, or 60 years of age? What makes these decade birthdays so important? Psychologists, who call them the big "0" birthdays (any age which ends in zero), are beginning to search for answers to these questions. So far, the evidence is preliminary, but it is beginning to suggest that the way we deal with big "0s" has an effect on the remainder of our lives.

There's no doubt about the fact that birthdays mark the passage of time. But decade-marking birth dates poignantly identify milestones in the aging process. As a result, it is impossible to escape the quasigifts or consequences which accompany a big "0" birthday. Like it or not, each big "0" — from 30 to 100 — comes with two presents: an extra dose of reality (which may have been denied over the past four or five years) and the requirement that individuals evaluate the quality of their lives to date.

Some people stay 29 years old forever — afraid, as Jonathan Swift said, to approach the "wrong side of 30." They have difficulty acknowledging that decades of their lives have passed. Big "0" birthdays force people to admit (at least in their own minds) the reality of their life cycles. Other numerical, non-zero birth years come and go; but it is impossible to deny a decade's passing.

The second inevitable consequence of the big "0" is introspection — sometimes negative. Birthdays in the 20th century have become occasions to explore thoughts, feelings, and aspirations. This is likely a holdover from Victorian times when children were given morality lessons on their birthdays. Additionally, bad birthdays were standard melodramatic themes in 19th-century fiction. Take the residual effect of these earlier times, combine it with modern fears generated by our youth-oriented culture, and it's surprising more people don't have trouble coping with birthdays — and aging in general.

When a big "0" birthday comes and goes, most people sit down and evaluate what they have accomplished. If they have not achieved their goals, they start to calculate how much time they have left to succeed. For some, this is a very positive time; for others, a most uncomfortable rite of passage. The way you deal with one big "0" determines how easily you will adjust to the others that follow.

The adjustment process associated with big "0s" has intrigued psychologists and sociologists for years. Freud wondered as to the secret of "these big round numbers." He concluded that successfully reaching these landmark birthdays represented "a measure of triumph over the transitoriness of life." However, later on in his life, he too, struggled with these decade birthdays. He said, "The way a man of 80 feels is not a fit subject for conversation." Reaching the big "0" milestone is certainly a measure of triumph over life, but how well one deals with each decade's big "0" characteristics is the real issue.

Consistent with the life cycle, big "0" decades have unique characteristics and generate many questions. Although research is currently limited, this area of study is beginning to emerge as an important one in developmental psychology. What is clear is that individuals moving through each decade exhibit certain personality characteristics.

Benjamin Franklin understood these demarcations when

he said, "At twenty years of age, the will reigns; at thirty, the wit; and at forty, the judgment." Franklin was right. However, with the rapid pace of technology and changes in the family structure, the adjustment process has become considerably more complicated.

Although Franklin talked about the big "0" at 20 years of age, psychologists are realizing that turning 20 is probably the least threatening for most people. Even though many lament that they are no longer teenagers, neither do they have the total responsibilities of full adulthood. They are free to satisfy their whims, and the requirements of others are subjugated. Within this time frame, 20-year-olds must come to realize that a certain freedom granted during childhood and adolescence is over. Within the next ten years, they will make many decisions and be called upon to evaluate them at age 30.

Perhaps the first big "0" which forces one to take stock of life is 30. As Franklin pointed out, reason begins to take over, and individuals become more "adult-like" — less playful, less spontaneous, and less flexible. They must, by cultural definition, be more serious. At this age, they begin to understand their mortality, and identify and evaluate their qualities and defects. New goals are formulated. Although there is a great deal of questioning at this age, it is not as provocative as in the approaching decades.

Research indicates that big "0s" tend to be more critical periods for women than men. Preliminary findings suggest that this is based on the fact that childbearing abilities and family demands change rapidly between 30 and 50. To take it a step further, ages 30 and 50 have been identified as the two most critical benchmarks for women.

Men, too, respond to these critical years, but in a way that may be surprising. At age 30, a slow role reversal begins between the sexes. As women age, they become more analytical, a prized masculine characteristic. As men age, they grow more emotional and less analytical. This is likely the result of the personal introspection which follows each big "0."

One other point about age 30 is that it is only five years away from age 35. Although 35 is not technically a big "0" year, there is anecdotal evidence that it is a milestone. Ask anyone who is turning 35, and he or she will admit to a great deal of questioning. They want to know: Do I look middle-aged? Do I feel middle-aged? Do I act my age? Women continue to be more concerned than ever with appearance; men begin to lose interest in their image.

Forty is the age at which people begin to see how obsessed they are with money and material success. Coincidentally, it is also the age which is considered the last possible chance to pull away from the crowd and create a name for one's self. Once again, values are questioned, with worries about being trapped and unable to do what one really wants to do. At age 40, the questions become more intense; physical changes more obvious; and emotions less controllable. In fact, the male/female roles begin to take on a definite shift. The female becomes more analytical as she evaluates her life; the male more compassionate.

Age 50 is a landmark year — a critical occasion for women, but it may not be for men. The person is living what Victor Hugo described: "Forty is the old age of youth, and fifty is the youth of old age."

At this level, dramatic physical changes prompt identity questions. Some even believe that this is a last-chance era. If individuals feel they have it together, they begin to relax and open themselves up to new thoughts, feelings, and emotions.

One important trademark of this age is that the individual is not as concerned about what others think of him or her. Overall, the 50-year-old is more willing to help others. There is also the fear that time is running out. As a result, it is not unusual for them to form stronger bonds or forge new ones to help them through the next big "0" birthday.

If 50 is a landmark year for women, then 60 is the critical milestone for men. The male can no longer kid himself, and now realizes what the female knew ten years ago. Acknowledging that he is in the "young-old" category, he is delighted to see that his vigor and stamina continue. At the same time, he notices many of his peers are looking old and unhealthy. The person is less concerned with money, and more desirous of comfort.

Once the person has made it over the 60-year benchmark successfully, there is evidence to suggest that, attitudinally, he or she is prepared for the ones that follow. They have worked through numerous crises and become more confident of their coping abilities.

To deal with the next big "0," it is necessary to develop affirmative attitudes, a set of positive behaviors, and to remember the following:

1. Mental powers need not decline with age. Verdi composed *Falstaff*, one of his greatest operas, at age 80. Winston Churchill retained power until he was 80. Pablo Picasso was drawing and engraving at age 90.

2. What you keep on doing, you can continue to do. Individuals who are considered elderly can perform complex tasks like playing chess or musical instruments even after other simpler abilities are gone. People who are active in their thirties and forties continue to be so even in middle age. Vladimir Horowitz, at the age of 81, returned to the Soviet Union for two concerts. Educator William J. Moore celebrated his 100th birthday recuperating from injuries sustained during a tennis match.

3. People who lead active lives when they are middle-aged tend to remain active through life. Physical and mental exer-

cise tend to keep the mind and body young. Practice, as shown in research, improves the skills of both young and old.

4. People with a positive attitude concerning aging continue to develop skills which may be considered appropriate for an earlier stage in life. For instance, Grandma Moses didn't become an artist until she was 76. Albert H. Gordon, Harvard class of 1923, ran his first marathon in 1982, at 80 years of age.

If you think that you may have trouble dealing with a big "0" birthday, there are several behavioral tricks you can use that will help you get through it.

Send yourself a birthday card, cake, flowers, and/or a present. When facing a big "0" birthday, most people try to deny it. This is not an effective birthday coping device. Denying a birthday only delays the reaction.

On a big "0" birthday, make sure to surround yourself with one or more friends with whom you can talk freely. Tell them your worries and concerns, and listen for their support.

Experiment with changing your image for a day (or longer, if you are up to it). Try a new hairstyle or add a distinctive piece of clothing to your wardrobe. Don't go overboard; keep it simple. If you are overly emotional about this birthday, do not make an expensive purchase. Buyer's remorse or guilt and worry about the birthday may be more than you can handle.

Plan an activity which you enjoyed earlier in life, but lately have not had time to do. First off, this takes your mind away from the birthday; and secondly, it takes you back to a time when you had fewer cares.

The key to dealing with a big "0" birthday has to do with your attitude going into it. Evaluate how you handled your last big "0," and prepare yourself mentally. If you expect the birthday to be rewarding, chances are it will be. Fears and worries can make the happiest of birthdays sad, but a change of attitude and behavior can minimize any problem.

References:
Niemela, P. & Kantola, R. 50 years as a turning point in women's lives. *Nordisk Psykologi*, 1982, *34*, pp. 257-266.

Notman, M.T. Women and mid-life: A different perspective. *Psychiatric Opinion*, 1978, *15*, pp. 15-25.

HOWDY, DOODLES!

Everybody doodles. Anyone who has ever put a felt-tip pen to paper has ultimately succumbed to that urge to instantly create a design, sketch, or scribble. But there's more to the maligned doodle than meets the eye; in fact, there is empirical evidence that may just elevate the "mindless" doodle to the status of "mindful" after all.

If you like to doodle, scrawl, scribble, or go where your pencil leads, you're in good company. Leonardo da Vinci doodled in the margins of his notebook. Fyodor Dostoyevski mixed doodling with the written word in his manuscripts. John F. Kennedy filled a page with the word "decesion" (sic) immediately prior to the Bay of Pigs confrontation. And President Reagan reportedly enjoys sketching human figures during committee meetings. Do these scribbles and scrawls mean anything? Maybe.

Virtually unnoticed for thousands of years, it was not until the 20th Century when Freud began his journey into the subconscious that the doodle became a candidate for interpretation. About the same time, the term "doodle" surfaced. The word supposedly gained popularity because of its use in the 1936 movie, *Mr. Deeds Goes to Town*. Almost overnight, the doodle was transformed from a pseudo-art form into a potential clue to the mysterious workings of the human psyche.

Now, many professional handwriting experts and graphologists are scrutinizing scribbles, scrawls, and doodles for parole boards, law enforcement agencies, and employers.

Although personality identification by doodling holds a certain mystique, the real question is: Does doodling play a role in personality development? The answer may surprise you. It *can* facilitate writing/spelling skills, social development, and even creativity.

To test the idea that doodling can improve writing and spelling skills, writing samples from 225 first-grade students were examined. In this experimental situation, students in a first-grade classroom were encouraged to scribble in conjunction with beginning attempts at writing. In addition, the students were told to use conventional orthography and make up a story. To give the experiment a twist, not only were students encouraged to use the alphabet and traditional words as they wrote their story, but they were also allowed to invent any other marks, scribbles, and symbols which would help in the preparation of the narrative.

Investigators found that students used scribbling and doodling in their writing for specific purposes and that scribbling served as a signal to the teacher that the child was ready for new knowledge. Not only did doodling help the child communicate a message, but it indirectly taught left-to-right directionality, manipulative control of the writing instrument, awareness of sentencing and spacing between words, and integrated the fun aspect of writing into work.

Further, another investigator gave personality tests to 96 elementary-school students. Several students were deficient in self-esteem or positive self-regard. Simply put, they were insecure. To resolve this problem, the insecure students were taught to write "d's" and "t's" with tall, thin stems and high crossbars. (Handwriting experts consider this a sign of self-confidence.) At the end of 30 days, personality tests were readministered. Supposedly due to the training, it was reported that 79 percent of the participants had improved their self-esteem.

Although this study did not report sophisticated statistical procedures or identify the probability of these results occurring by chance, the finding is still interesting. If a child is encouraged and taught during the formative period to increase the number of doodles and to expand the scribble's size, would this be an additional tool in a parent's bag of tricks for helping their children develop positive socialization skills? Evidence suggests that this commonsense approach is capable of improving interaction.

In another experiment, 76 female undergraduate subjects were involved in determining if the size of the doodle is related to personality variables like introversion/extroversion and degree of anxiety. Since an introvert prefers a small circle of friends and is sometimes rather shy around people, and an extrovert enjoys many friends and must be the center of attention, it follows that the extrovert's doodles are much larger, or expansive, than those created by the introvert. However, when anxiety was measured along with extroversion and introversion, the findings were reversed.

What happens to the size of the extrovert's doodle when he or she is depressed, anxious, or worried? As expected, the anxious extrovert's doodles shrunk in size when compared to nonanxious extroverts. What happens to the size of the introvert's doodle when anxiety becomes a factor? Does it become smaller? If you guessed that the worried introvert's drawings also grew smaller, guess again. The exact opposite occurred. The anxious introvert created larger drawings than his nonanxious introverted friends. Furthermore, the anxiety-ridden extrovert's doodles became *smaller* than the shy, anxious introvert's scribblings. The explanation here is that anxiety obviously takes its toll. But what accounts for the opposite reaction? How does it translate into a real-life situation?

Assuming that the presence of anxiety is a signal that something is wrong, the human psyche will try to remove the painful feelings. When a problem surfaces, extroverts, who recognize anxiety as a danger signal and who perceive themselves as having everything to lose, overwithdraw or back off in an attempt to minimize their possible losses. They constrict or restrict their range of behaviors. The smaller doodle is one example. On the other hand, introverts, who also recognize anxiety as a symptom of an impending problem and who perceive themselves as having little to lose, become more active or expansive as a means of coping, addressing the problem, and finding a solution. As a result, in anxious times, their typical doodle grew larger.

Whether child or adult, introvert or extrovert, if you're creative, then your doodle has a definite, distinctive style. As a general rule, the creative man or woman's doodle demonstrates complexity, as opposed to simplicity — drawings tend to be asymmetrical, dynamic, and chaotic. One theory suggests that creative individuals overincorporate, take in, and utilize information which others would call extraneous or superfluous. Just as creative individuals tend to process more information than needed, so do they demonstrate this in their free-thinking doodles. Active doodling, creating more and more complex designs, allowing the brain to absorb complexity, may be one technique for improving one's creative skills. Even if it doesn't improve creativity, doodling can be fun — and attempting to interpret its various meanings can be revealing.

Scientific evidence aside, some practicing graphoanalysts believe that doodles reveal oodles about personality. Unfortunately, doodle and handwriting analyses have not been verified by hard statistical data. However, there are anecdotal results which are fun and provide a preliminary clue to the inner workings of personality. The following are presented for fun and meant only to entertain.

Have you ever caught yourself repeatedly drawing arrows, race cars, running animals, stars, words, your spouse's name, or human figures? Or perhaps you repeat geometrical shapes — angular boxes, circles, or triangles. What type of pencil or pen do you prefer? Do you color or shade portions of the doodle? Handwriting experts believe that the answers to these questions may reveal your deepest secrets.

If you regularly draw arrows, then you are expressing your need for ambition (if the arrows point up). Race cars and running animals suggest a desire to run away or escape from your current living pattern. Stars express hope. Scribbling words all over a page is a sure sign of an intellectual (remember the Kennedy example). The doodling of faces and human figures suggests a sociable personality.

What about deeper emotions? These are usually expressed by angular or tangled horizontal lines. Such doodles suggest hidden anger and frustration. Symmetrical, detailed doodles are drawn by very precise individuals who pride themselves on their conformity. These individuals are usually intolerant of chaos and insist on planning everything to the last possible detail. Deep, dark shading may suggest anxieties and worries; preference for bright colors suggests a person who expresses emotion.

The writing tool also provides another clue. Those who desire to be evasive will usually select a pencil; it has an eraser, and if you change your mind, it leaves no traces. Felt-tip doodlers usually want to be the center of attention and like to make a strong first impression with the least amount of work. A regular pen is the instrument of choice for those individuals who are capable of keeping their egos in check.

Simply put, doodling — aimless or not — is a creative outlet. It doesn't require any thinking, because there are no right or wrong answers. In fact, doodling is a common denominator. From the boardroom to the desk blotter, it's something we *all* do...

References:

Heald-Taylor, B.G. Scribble in first grade writing. *Reading Teacher,* 1984, *38*, pp. 4-8.

Kernan, M. The nation's scrapbook: On the archives' 50th, presidential doodles and royal recipes. *Washington Post,* June 20, 1984, *107*, B1.

Leo, J. The customers always write. Time, September 6, 1982, *120*, p. 80.

Wallach, M.A., & Gahm, R.C. Personality functions of graphic constriction and expansiveness. *Journal of Personality,* 1960, *28*, pp. 73-88.

WINDS OF CHANGE

It used to be that the Great American Pastime was baseball. Not necessarily so any more. There's a new pastime sweeping the nation, and it's called "change."

On the up side, people see change as a problem solver. In order to get out of a bad situation, hundreds of thousands of people will change jobs this year. Moreover, approximately forty million of us will change our addresses. And more will attempt to change their personalities, spouses, and (most of all) the kids.

Unfortunately, there is a down side to change, and it involves unexpected changes, or those things which are difficult to control. In fact, there are some who believe that too much of either positive or negative change can lead to physical and emotional problems. There is even evidence that change may cause our internal biological clocks to malfunction.

This biological clock produces 24-hour rhythmic fluctuations observable in the metabolic processes of both plants and animals. These cycles, called "circadians" (from the Latin meaning "about the day"), are not the same as "biorhythms," which occur over a period of days. Circadians are very strong, essential to daily living, and tend to remain constant. These biological rhythms hardly fluctuate, even if you are cut off from all means of discerning day from night over a period as long as several months. However, as anyone who has ever crossed too many time zones in too short a time knows, rapid change will disrupt the process that requires the body to reset its biological clock.

Although these daily body rhythms are invisible, they relate to sleep, chemical constituents in the blood, hormone production, and temperature. For instance, body temperature tends to rise around seven in the morning and decrease around ten at night. Any abrupt change, causing a disruption of this daily rhythmic flow, may result in physical malfunction.

Empirical studies of disturbances in circadian cycles in humans (e.g., sudden change in sleep cycles) have shown that adaptability varies greatly from person to person. In experiments with simulated manned space flight, some participants responded well to unusual work schedules (work four hours; rest four hours). Other participants had great difficulty adapting and coping. One very interesting point must be made: changes that the activities demanded of each subject did not vary from situation to situation. Each participant in the study was required to do the same thing. What did vary was the individual's ability to adapt, cope, and reset his or her biological clock. Change may not be the culprit that produces problems; but rather, the individual's ability to adapt to change.

Over the past 30 years, a great deal of evidence has suggested that the number of changes — controllable and uncontrollable, positive and negative — which occur in a person's life are related to illness. To measure this, certain life events have been given numerical values and are referred to as "life-change units." Examples of life changes include loss of a loved one, jail term, marriage, job termination, birth of a child, mortgages, holidays, family get-togethers, and others. Research has suggested that the greater number of these "life changes" experienced in a period of time (usually one year), the greater the probability of one's becoming sick. The more changes, the more vulnerable one's immune system becomes.

These vanguard studies have pointed out that change takes its toll; however, more recent studies are suggesting that life change does not necessarily have to be debilitating or even associated with illness. The key to minimizing the harmful effects of positive and negative change appears to be resiliency — the ability to bounce back and effectively deal with, and adapt to, the effects of change. The real question then becomes: what is it that allows one person to bounce back effectively, and yet another who experiences the same life change to fall apart? The answer is related to the person's age and his or her expectations.

To test this idea, a study was conducted among undergraduate students. The study surveyed 87 male and 91 female undergraduates (between 18 and 30 years of age). The experimenters were looking for a relationship between life events which caused change and the prevalence of emotional problems. After administering a written survey which measured the number of life-change units over the past year, it was found that 84.8 percent of the subjects had scores indicative of major life crises. To see if the participants also admitted to corresponding sickness or emotional problems, another scale was administered. Given the high percentage of stressful events in the students' lives, the experimenters expected to find a pronounced level of sickness. That's not what happened.

Though much change occurred in their lives, there was very little evidence of physical disorders. Only modest experimental support justified this conclusion that change and illness are related. In this group of subjects, change did not necessarily lead to emotional distress or illness.

This case contradicts other studies conducted with adults, which have shown that a great deal of life change can predispose one to physical and emotional problems. What caused the opposite results? One theory attributes the outcome to the participants, combined with the fact that the undergraduates would not allow illness to interfere as they progressed toward their goals in college. To further test the idea that one's ability to cope is related to age and life goals, let's take a look at the next example.

A similar study was done with an older population. This study was composed of 132 men and 167 women over the age of 65. They completed a battery of tests designed to examine the relationship between life changes for each gender and vulnerability to illness. One other very important variable was assessed: the examiners also wanted to know if a person's coping resources played a part in adjusting to change.

The result suggested that older women responded more to change than older males. This is not an unusual finding, given the fact that women tend to express more emotion than men. The fact that excessive change is related to illness was also supported.

Even more interesting was the experimenters' findings that the usual coping techniques were not effective when related to the largely negative and uncontrollable events of old age. Having a marriage partner, confidante, or a strong self-concept were not effective aids in coping with excessive life change. As a result, the more uncontrollable life changes associated with aging at a rapid rate, combined with inhibited coping skills, contributed to the likelihood of illness.

Although the undergraduates cited earlier experienced many life changes, they admitted to little emotional distress. The 65- year-old groups were experiencing an increase in illness and emotional distress in conjunction with an increase in life changes. Although there were significant differences in the age groups, these two studies suggest that it is not change which is causing the problem, but the ability to cope and to adapt to change. When one is young, with pristine goals upon which to focus, the effects of change are more easily minimized. As one ages, with more and more accumulated failures and less time to achieve, change takes its toll.

There is no doubt that accelerated change has played havoc with our established norms and values. The rate and pervasiveness of change today is totally different from anything our ancestors ever experienced. Every facet of our lives is affected by change. Our educational system, jobs, family lives, leisure pursuits, economic positions, beliefs, and values are constantly in flux.

In the early 1970s, the concept of "future shock" emerged to describe a condition whereby social change would be exceedingly rapid. The result was expected to be profound confusion and emotional pain. Change which is too rapid produces "techno- stress," or the inability to adjust and to bounce back at a commensurate pace. However, there are ways to deal with this problem.

There are three important points to remember: change can be minimized; belief in future goals reduces the deleterious effects of change; and , at the risk of sounding redundant, the way to deal with change is to change.

The most effective way to minimize change is through planning. If you are anticipating a relocation, start preparing several months in advance. Talk with people who have moved; take copious notes; write things down so that you will not forget the details. By doing this, you are making unfamiliar things seem more in line with your current regimen of behavior. The more understanding you have of a soon-to-happen event, the less debilitating change will be. First-graders who visit school several days before they start adjust better. Surgery patients who are thoroughly familiar with what is to happen heal faster. Visit a new city several times before your move. The more you know about a change, the less intimidating it is.

If you think that you are at the mercy of change, or that you have minimal control over a situation, then you are making yourself vulnerable to potential physical and emotional problems. If you are enduring a change in order to reach a higher plateau, or to fulfill expectations and desires, then the effects of change are overshadowed. Your goals and future orientation give you a reason for putting up with the hassles. By focusing on the positive goal, you are impervious to the negative side effects of change. For instance, remember the young undergraduates who were content with their role as students. Focusing on obtaining a college degree reduced the negative effects of change and made them less vulnerable to illness.

Finally, the most effective way to deal with change is to change. Readjust your thinking and respond with positive action. Most of the problems associated with change stem from fear and inability to develop a plan of attack. We get so caught up in life changes that it becomes very difficult to view the circumstances objectively. Because we do not know what will happen to us, we tend to blow situations out of proportion. The more negative your thinking concerning upcoming and/or unseen changes, the greater the probability of not adjusting well to change. If you are anticipating a change, get the facts straight. Become familiar with the problem, and never lose sight of your goals.

The bottom line is that change is not all bad, but it is inevitable, and one of the few constants in daily living. You can't change that, but you can change your outlook on it. That's the first step in effectively coping with change.

References:
Cole, G.E. Life change events as stressors and their relationship to mental health among undergraduate university students. *Psychological Reports,* 1985, 56, pp. 387-390.

West, G.E., & Simons, R.L. Sex differences in stress, coping resources, and illness among the elderly. *Research on Aging,* 1983, 5, pp. 235-268.

BODY TALK

Have you ever said something and no one listened? Then the person sitting next to you said the exact same thing, and everyone thought it was a great idea. Perhaps you've wondered why no heads turn when you enter the room. Better yet, do you always lose at competition because your face gives you away? The problem may be not in what you say, but how your body says it.

The body has a language of its own. And, of course, psychologists have a name for it: kinesics, informally referred to as body language. Simply, kinesics is the study of communication through body movements, gestures, and facial expressions. You may have seen it referred to as "meta-talk."

First, a disclaimer. Researchers in this field emphasize that gestures are rarely fixed in meaning. Facial and body gestures add emotional expression to what is spoken. Moreover, if you can spot the discrepancy between what is said and what is indicated by body language, then you quite possibly have the potential to become the greatest salesman in the world, or the most astute manager in your field.

The face is most usually noticed. In fact, your face is capable of producing over 20,000 expressions, or facial blends. That "come hither" look is only one of the lot. Say, for instance, that you just got an "F" on a test, or a performance report was low, or some unexpected failure has just occurred. Your eyes, eyebrows, and forehead will express anger. But your mouth will give you away. It will express sadness. The upper part of your face is trying to hide the hurt through anger, but the mouth is telling the truth. Behind every angry facade is a hurt little boy or girl.

The smile can be an interesting paradox. Let's say that someone is really giving you a hard time, but is smiling while doing so. See what the smile did? It added the element of confusion. You have difficulty judging the degree of insult. By smiling, the emotional messages of pleasantness and acceptance have been added to a verbal insult. The entire communication has been changed. There is indeed a message in the Old West adage, "Smile when you say that, pardner."

Do body positioning or facial expressions reveal lying and deception? Not usually. The reason for this is that most people are able to maintain careful control over their facial expressions. For example, as every bride-and groom-to-be know, there are just so many blenders needed in one household. However, upon receiving the fifth blender, one must act as excited as the time when the first kitchen appliance was received. So what do you do? You fake it. The deception will not be realized in the face because you will control yourself to avoid hurting the giver and to increase the likelihood that when the first child is born you will receive another present (face it, that's human nature). The deception can be observed by the lower body. Tense leg positions, and restless or repetitive foot and leg movements are associated with fibbing. Even a good con artist is usually too busy attending to a "poker face" to exert control over the other areas.

One final point about the face. Never forget that the eyes dilate when pleasing things are seen, and constrict when the situation is the opposite. So if your gift had been appropriate, the face would have lit up with a big smile, eyes dilated, and lower body parts not fidgeted.

Overall body tone is easily communicated by body language. Take relaxation, for instance. Relaxation is expressed by casual positioning of arms and legs, leaning back (if sitting), and spreading of arms and legs. An air of openness is communicated. In other words, the individual is encouraging you to approach and to interact. Uptight bodies are rigid and straightbacked. When people are more relaxed, they tend to "hang loose."

However, even the dullest individual is aware of the body message which says "hands off." Take the individual who stands rigidly, crosses his/her arms over the chest, and sits with legs tightly crossed. There is little doubt that this person is sending a "don't invade my space" message. Body language is only one way that people assert their independence.

Personal space is both protective and communicative. Anxious people position themselves farther away than the non-anxious. To elaborate, people seek a safe distance from others when escape or an exit could be a problem. Notice the space between interactions. Intimate interactions require approximately one and a half feet or less; close friends interact between four and 12 feet; and performers to audience, lawyer to judge, and other more formal situations require at least 12 feet.

Individuals tend to stand nearer to people of the same race, age, and socioeconomic level. They tend to come closer as the interaction increases. But there are differences in the way genders respond. Men still pile books protectively in front of them when working in libraries or at their desk; women tend to spread them out.

Then there's the question of touching. Women are more capable of emotionally responding to a touch; men's blood pressure tends to increase when they are touched. There is evidence to support the fact that a touch is an effective adjunct to other body language cues in asking for help.

One study was done in which a female, who appeared distressed, asked for dimes to make a phone call. When she lightly touched the person whom she was asking for money on the arm, her request was usually honored. In other words, she received more dimes.

It's very easy to tell if a person is saying "Get out of my face."

But how do you know if they want to initiate an interaction with you? Liking is expressed by leaning toward a person or object. That's an important point to remember. Let's say that you are trying to make a sale or close an important deal, but the individual is giving you no facial clues. How do you know when the individual is beginning to see it your way? Watch for them to lean toward you. Additionally, they will probably start giving more eye contact. People who like what they are hearing or seeing tend to gaze more and to lean forward. If you want to know if your mate really loves you, observe the amount of time they spend leaning toward you and gazing "lovingly" into your eyes. If the individual avoids eye contact, you may want to evaluate the possibility of deception.

Now, before you start attempting to read body language, here's a trial run: take a snapshot out of your wallet or purse. A picture is a great way to garner an understanding of body language. With picture in hand, ask yourself the following questions: How are the people in the picture grouped — who's standing next to whom? Who is touching whom? Is one person always in the center of the photograph? Is your father- or mother-in-law hovering over you? Who isn't in the picture? Who was left out? Are people gazing lovingly at each other, or is there hate in their eyes and a smile on their lips? Is the pet in the picture used to keep people away?

A picture is worth more than a 1,000 words. In fact, photographs can divulge body language in a surprisingly powerful way. By answering the above questions and systematically observing, you will be surprised what you find out about the people you think that you know.

Finally, another point about body language has to do with first appearances. Like it or not, first appearances are extremely important. That's why you wear your best clothes for a job interview, or why attorneys outfit their clients before they are seen by a jury. We learn at an early age that the way people dress and carry themselves are important clues as to how they think, feel, and behave.

However, the most sophisticated clothing in the world can't help you if your body language contradicts your dress. As Professor Higgins taught Eliza Dolittle in *My Fair Lady,* dress, speech, manners, and carriage all combine to create a human countenance called "body language." One must make sure that these four areas all say the same thing.

In effect, if you can't say it with flowers, and words fail you, try body talk. That always gets their attention.

References:

Coon, D. *Introduction to Psychology.* New York: West Publishing Company, 1983.

Fast, J. *Body Language,* New York: M. Evans, 1970.

Fenjves, P. Snapshots on the couch. *Omni,* 1984, *6*, p. 8.

Karabenick, S.A., & Meisels, M. Effects of performance evaluation on interpersonal distance. *Journal of Personality,* 1972, *40*, pp. 275-286.

Mehrabian, A. Significance of posture and position in the communication of attitude and status relationships. *Psychological Bulletin*, 1969, *71*, pp. 359-372.

Swenson, C.H. *Introduction to Human Relations*, Glenview, Illinois: Scott, Foresman, 1973.

GETTING IT TOGETHER

There's more to getting organized than simply completing a "To Do" list. In fact, time management alone is not a conscious act. There are unseen forces which influence how we structure our lives. These hidden, almost unconscious behaviors tip the scales between frustration and fulfillment, pleasure and pain.

Most of us go about our lives in the same way each day and allow these unseen powers to have full control. In an attempt to change and to become more productive, millions of dollars are spent each year on self-help time-management books. Although they offer excellent advice and valuable techniques, many fail to mention the role that unseen influences, like perception of time and personal priorities, play in the overall organizational balance. When these two areas are better understood, the role of time management as part of everyday living is much easier to assimilate.

The perception of time is a critical, yet often overlooked issue in time management. Most people don't think of themselves as past-, present-, or future-oriented. Yet, psychologists know that this is an important variable. One's view of the past, present, or future is an unseen determinant of one's willingness to organize and manage time.

A recent study by the American Psychological Association surveyed over 10,000 people in the U.S., Puerto Rico, and the Virgin Islands. Participants were asked to describe their time perspective — for example, whether they think more about the past, present, or future. From the sample, 57 percent chose a balance between present and future, 33 percent were more future- oriented, nine percent were present-focused, and one percent preferred to live in the past. Those with future orientations considered themselves "planners"; individuals with present orientations lived in the moment and, by choice, avoided planning or thinking ahead.

When occupations were compared to temporal preferences, the results directly relate to time management. As you would expect, managers, teachers, and other white-collar types were more future-oriented. Semiskilled individuals were more present- centered.

Time perspective has a direct bearing on one's perception of the need for time management. The time-orientation exerts either a motivational push toward success or a pull toward complacency. A future-oriented individual in a managerial position understands goals, deadlines, and the need to squeeze a lot into very little time. Someone with a present or past perspective placed in a managerial position, no matter how many time-management classes he or she takes, may never quite grasp the complexities of getting organized.

Although temporal or time perspective is important, there is also another unseen area which influences how time is organized. Psychologists refer to this component as a "priority base."

Most of us tend to have one important base, or focus, around which our time-management decisions are made. If work is the priority and perceived as more important than home, then time- management decisions will benefit office first, and leftover time will be reserved for home.

Everyone has a target, priority base, or frame of reference around which time-management decisions are formulated. People organize around space, people, work, home, and other obligations. One research study evaluated the priority-planning patterns of 120 adults. Through an interview, questionnaire, and other self- report techniques, four priority-based areas emerged: home; work; home/work combination; and social/extra-curricular.

Researchers found that individuals who are home-based organize in a way that maximizes their time at home with their family. They do not do less work than their colleagues; however, if there is an opportunity to manage a group of activities to give them time at home, they will do so. These people tend to be married and place a high value on time spent with family. Many were self- employed or in jobs which allowed them to work from their homes. Compared to the other three groups, these "homebodies" tend to be happier and more satis-fied.

Individuals who organize their time around work obvious-ly spend a great deal of time in that environment. Work is clearly the center of their personal universe. Not only is their work of high quality, but high quantity as well. As a result, they make more money than the three other groups. Their lives tend to be fast-paced. If they are single and male, they tend to spend large amounts of time at work and are less happy than any of the other three groups.

Those individuals who have a balance between work and home rarely do anything else. Their management decisions are not as prejudiced as those who prefer either home to office or vice versa. They are managing their time in a way which gives them the best of both worlds. Research suggests both work at home and office is characterized by both quality and quantity, with little differentiation.

Finally, there are those who organize their life with little thought of home or office. These people prioritize sporadical-ly, based on diffuse social responsibilities. No one place forms the center of their world. They express neither high quality nor quantity time at home or work. Rather, they float and prefer to organize their time around social activities which are spon-taneous, diverse, and numerous. Generally speaking, this group tends to be less content with their life than any of the others. Because there is no single focus, priority, or base, these people tend to have more of a problem managing time.

Just as there are indirect influences on how we manage time, there are also very powerful direct and conscious tech-niques which maximize time usage. These procedures work for all orientations and their successful implementation provides more time to spend on priority wants and needs. They consist of tried-and-true behavioral routines which, when used properly, allow you to manage time instead of allowing time to rule you.

Whether at home or the office, 80 percent of your time will be taken up by the system (meetings, telephone calls, paperwork, housework, child care). A routine of behavioral methods and tricks are essential to effectively manage a day's work in 20 percent of the time. Although most of these tricks are designed for the office, some slight modifications will make them work at home as well.

Start with the morning mail. Most time-management experts agree that the best technique is the "A-B-C Method." Prioritize it as follows: Write the letter "A" in the top right margin if the letter requires an immediate reply; "B" if the response can be handled through dictation; and "C" if it is low-priority reading which can be done later in the day or on the commute home.

Implement the "A-B-C Method" as a means of delegation. When you assign projects for completion, inform your staff of the following code: An "A" project is a "Don't do anything until I've authorized it"; "B" means "Get on with it, and let me know afterwards what you did"; and "C" is "Get on with it, and I don't need to know what happened." This method stops interruptions before they happen. Anything you can do to avoid interruptions means improved time management. It has been estimated that a one-minute interruption can cost as long as 20 minutes to rebuild your momentum.

Instead of allowing paperwork to pile higher and higher on your desk, have a series of work trays labeled, "Do next," "Read," "Pass for Filing," "See secretary," "Dictation," and "Awaiting information." Use these trays, and never have more than one piece of information or project on your desk at a time.

If you are working on a project or letter, don't stop until you reach a legitimate point of closure. Research studies show that if you stop a project prematurely by saying, "I'll get back to it," you probably will not. If you must stop something before resolving the issue, give yourself a definite time and date to get back to it. Mark that new date on your calendar.

Set aside two, 30-minute "red" times each day. Mark them in red on your calendar, and inform your staff and all those around you that you are unavailable. Close your door, and make this time as productive as possible. Avoid phone calls during this period.

Group your phone calls and place them either 30 minutes before lunch or closing. This will minimize the other person's wanting to "chit-chat," so you can get straight to the point.

Outline in writing what you plan to accomplish tomorrow. If you use a "To Do" list, make the items as specific as possible. Break the job down into a number of small components. Instead of "Cleaning office files," be specific and change it to read, "Discard outdated papers." Use the "A-B-C" method and code each listed job for urgency. Do the "A's" first and "C's" last.

Finally, no matter how much you enjoy your office or work, end the day with some type of divertisement. The most effective organizers know when to take a "mental-health break." This will give you the extra momentum you need for tomorrow.

To get better organized, then, you need to know three things. First, your time perspective. Next, identify the target, focus, or needs around which you organize your daily list of activities. Finally, implement behavior-change techniques which maximize your current organizational and time-management skills. The result is better future planning and resolved priorities. In other words, to manage time, you must first manage yourself.

References:

Gonzalez, A., & Zimbardo, P. Time in perspective. *Psychology Today,* 1985, *19,* pp. 21-26.

Jensen, K. How to have your cake and get to eat it, too. *Canadian Business,* September, 1985, p. 164.

Lee, M.D. The great balancing act. *Psychology Today,* 1986, *20,* pp. 48-55.

Lee, M.D. Life space structure; explorations and speculations. *Human Behavior*, 1985, *38*, pp. 623-642.

THE POWERS THAT BE

The notion of power is ubiquitous; there's an element of power in everything we see and do. It is essential in handling and managing those aspects of our lives that can, on occasion, get out of control. Whether it is losing weight, supervising others, or making the advent of old age more productive, it basically boils down to dominating areas of our behavior.

There are two aspects of power: 1. Power used to control and manipulate others; and 2. Personal power, which we use in controlling our own lives. Power used effectively is, of course, a positive force. The problem comes when power is allowed to grow out of control and to take on a negative, manipulative cast.

The concept of negative control over others is nothing new. Sophocles discussed it and noted strong psychological ramifications. In fact, manipulative power is the sort of notion upon which good novels, plays, television dramas, and newspaper stories are built.

Shakespeare's plays are textbook examples. One researcher counted the number of instances of "tough control" or power (orders, threats, angry outbursts) in two of Shakespeare's plays. In *King Lear,* there were approximately 150 instances of "control by force." In the more popular *Macbeth,* the number doubled. There were 267 specific examples of direct orders and threats designed to control others.

It doesn't matter if it's King Lear, Macbeth, a person dominating a spouse, or an executive overcontrolling an organization — when one person exerts excessive power and

forces a subordinate to act, three negative psychological ingredients or personality traits will emerge.

J. R. Ewing of television's *Dallas* has these three essential
psychological components which fascinate us all.

First, he freely exploits others. He sees people as objects
rather than human beings. Second, and as a direct result of his
habitually and successfully controlling others, he is "puffed up"
with his own importance. His ego is out of control, fed by his
own feelings of self-grandeur. Third, his moral values are those
which serve his purpose — not necessarily those fostered or encouraged by the culture. In other words, in his own mind, he
justifies what he does based on *his* definition of what is moral.

Not everyone exerts power as mercilessly as J.R., King
Lear, or Macbeth. In addition to "power by force," there are
two other approaches: soft-sell and factual techniques.

People who use "soft sell" to get you to do things their way
are usually described as "nice." They prefer flattery and pleading rather than direct demands or orders. They make you think
that you are doing them a favor.

If that approach does not work, they may try the factual
technique. The factual approach consists of explaining, discussing, and compromising. It appeals to your reason: "Isn't
this the sensible thing to do?" If you disagree, you look as if
you are the fool; as a result, you do what is asked. If you do not
acquiesce, power by force may be the only remaining option —
and the most popular one.

Unfortunately, most power wielders like to throw their
weight around. They do this by ordering, threatening, and getting angry. You do what they want either because you're afraid,
or so that the person will calm down. Threats, orders, and
temper are used to control resources, emotions, and/or finances needed or valued by another person. When the would-be
power source identifies your "Achilles' heel," then he or she

has the advantage in the relationship, whether it is commercial or personal.

Which of the three approaches is used most often? People with power who are sensitive to the needs of their subordinates may not use hard tactics as their first choice. They may make a request. If it is not carried out, they then resort to demands and threats. People with little power tend to start obstreperously and immediately shift to softer tactics (pleading and begging) when they encounter resistance. As you would expect, however, the greater the discrepancy or difference in clout, chain of command, or administrative responsibility between the power-holder and the target, the more likely that hard tactics are used with no explanation.

Although shouts and demands may make people move faster, they have harmful side effects for both the recipient and the power- holder.

Simply put, people evaluate others less favorably when they perceive that they are controlled by forces outside themselves. The person who is controlled is devalued. This sets the stage for even more exploitation.

For example, in a recent study of 195 couples (76 married and 119 dating), partners were asked to describe how they made the other person do what they wanted. What tactic (soft, factual, or force) did they use to get their way? Examples of answers depicting the three power approaches were: "My partner has the final say," "We both decide," and "I have the final say."

The findings suggested that partners who use strong techniques to control the other also believed that they had the final word. Those who used more rational or factual tactics reported they shared the decision-making. Those who used weaker techniques tended to allow the other partner to make the decisions and hold the power. But these expected findings were not the most interesting. An unexpected result emerged concerning how power influences the degree and level of affection between couples.

Would you think that having an overly compliant partner or group of employees would promote harmony and affection? Not so. People who were identified as "controlling" or "holding the power" had a less rewarding relationship than those who shared power. Once the seat of power was firmly established, the dominant partner became disenchanted and bored with the relationship. As a result, the controlling partner described his or her partner in less flattering terms and devalued their intelligence, success, and skill. They also expressed less love for their partner.

Unfortunately, this makes psychological sense. The partner or employee who is submissive is not allowed to exhibit competence. As a result, the person who makes the decisions takes all the credit and views the other person as useless. Therefore, dominance and power are negatively associated with positive regard and feelings of affection toward the target of the power.

These findings transfer to the workplace as well. The same researchers appointed 200 business students to serve as managers of work groups whose task was to assemble small model cars. The leaders were instructed to manage using either a forceful/authoritarian technique or factual/democratic approach. The forceful leaders had total control over all decisions; the democratic leaders shared power with the group workers.

The study revealed that the employees working for both types of leaders did equally good work. However, the most interesting findings came when the leaders were asked to evaluate the employees.

The leaders who held the power through authoritarian means and used a forceful technique, devalued their group employees. They stated that the participants did not work hard, nor was their work of high quality. Once again, the dominant person made all decisions — what to do, and how and when to do it. As a result, they did not attribute any good work to the employees' skills and talents. If the people did as they were told, their behavior was attributed to the power-holder's orders. Subordinate persons received no credit for what they accomplished effectively. Only when there was a mistake or error did the authoritarian leader allow the participant to take credit.

The more a person is involved in routine, nonthinking, automatic tasks, the more likely he or she will be devalued either in the home or on the assembly line. If the required behavior is difficult, nonroutine, or specialty work, you have the edge. In technical-specific duties, poor performance is rarely blamed on the worker's abilities. Work difficulty, equipment failure, or even the need for more training are seen as the culprits. The key here is to become indispensable. Then, the power source is less likely to devalue that employee, partner, or spouse.

What about personal control and willpower? The same principles apply. Whether it's losing an extra ten pounds or increasing productivity at the office, it's a question of power over yourself. Remember the following rules:

1. Willpower and self-control, just like any other aspect of physical and psychological health, must be exercised often. As William James, American psychologist and champion of self-control, pointed out: "Acts of will... cannot be inattentively performed. A distinct idea of what they are, and a deliberate 'fiat' on the mind's part, must precede their execution."

2. Where there is want, there is power. If you want something badly, find the power inside you to achieve it. First, decide what it is you want to control; how badly you want to control it; then create an objective plan of attack. Your strategy should focus on controlling all resources, finances, and

emotions essential to achieving control and gaining power over what you want.

3. When possible, alter routine. Find novel ways to do things. In searching for new procedures and techniques, you give added meaning to what you are doing or attempting to control.

4. Keep communication channels open within yourself. Use the three tactics of power to talk to yourself and to control your own behavior. Flatter yourself when it's appropriate; use objective facts often as a means of deciding on appropriate ways to behave; threaten and punish yourself when you consciously veer off course.

5. Anticipate consequences. Recognize in advance those situations in which you have total control, limited control, or none at all. By doing this, you can anticipate consequences and better plan a strategy to deal with a potential problem or power- holder. The more accurately you can guess what will happen, the more in control you will be.

6. You always have the power to say "No!" You determine the degree to which another person exerts control over you. If you are the target of an individual's power trip, remember that you are giving them that power. The more you acquiesce to their demands, the greater their ego is inflated at your expense. The more you give in, the greater the likelihood that you will devalue yourself.

7. Finally, "earn" the right to be powerful. Powerful people achieve control over themselves and others as a result of mutual respect. The truly powerful use honesty and integrity in dealing with themselves, family, children, business associates, and friends. The end result is an honest self-esteem, rather than a false, inflated ego.

References:
Blanchard, K. Jelly bean motivation, *Success,* February 1986, p.8.

James. W. *The Will to Believe,* New York. Longmans, Green, and Company, 1899.

Kipnis, D., & Schmidt, S. The language of persuasion. *Psychology Today,* April 1985, pp. 40-46.

Kipnis, D. The view from the top. *Psychology Today*, December 1984, pp. 30-36.

ADDITIONAL COPIES AVAILABLE

<u>YOUR BEHAVIOR IS SHOWING</u>
by
PERRY W. BUFFINGTON, PH.D.

To order copies of this dynamic book by Dr. Buffington, fill out the form below and mail it with your check or money order (made payable to Hillbrook House) to:

Hillbrook House

3737 Hillbrook Court

Nashville, TN 37211

Please send me _____ copies of <u>Your Behavior Is Showing</u> at $9.95 each plus $1.75 postage and handling per order. Tennessee residents add $.60 tax per book.

Enclosed is my check or money order for $ _____.

Please print or type:

Name: _____

Address: _____

City/State/Zip: _____